Deshi Dreams

Literature from the Creative Writing in English Course
March 3 – April 4, 2006
Presidency University
Dhaka, Bangladesh

"The First Day of Class"

Published by
Wayward Bride Press
in cooperation with
Trafford Publishing

Order this book online at www.trafford.com
or email orders@trafford.com

Most Trafford titles are also available at major online book retailers.

Print information available on the last page.

ISBN: 978-1-4251-0834-2 (sc)

Trafford rev. 12/01/2020

www.trafford.com

North America & international
toll-free: 844-688-6899 (USA & Canada)
fax: 812 355 4082

Class Snapshots

Sameeha and Mahreen   Shaima, Nur, Nadia, and Nasrin

Alipha and Parsa   Hildi and Bushra

Parsa, Kashfi, Akhter, and Alipha Bushra, Hildi, Idrak, Sarmad, and Walid

Kashfi Ahmed

Kashfi was standing on the stage. She seemed very nervous but internally she was is feeling great to out here. Hundreds of people were crowding infront of her. It was her big moment. She ...

Creative Writing Student

Your Name: KASHFI AHMED

What name would you like me to use for you in class? KASHFI

Picture:

Vinny, sitting in the front ... with a gentle smile, he watched ... His mind was into somethi... A lives together kept distrac... He had sacrificed immense... busy in her world of writi... go on for months. He re they... and Kashfi was glad to ... been of great support and ... that Vinny did for her kept ... may sound crazy but Kashfi ... Vinny would often get h... liquid. He would do almost everything for her despite his ...

Akhter Jahan

Autobiography, Biography & Memoir:
A Golden Delight

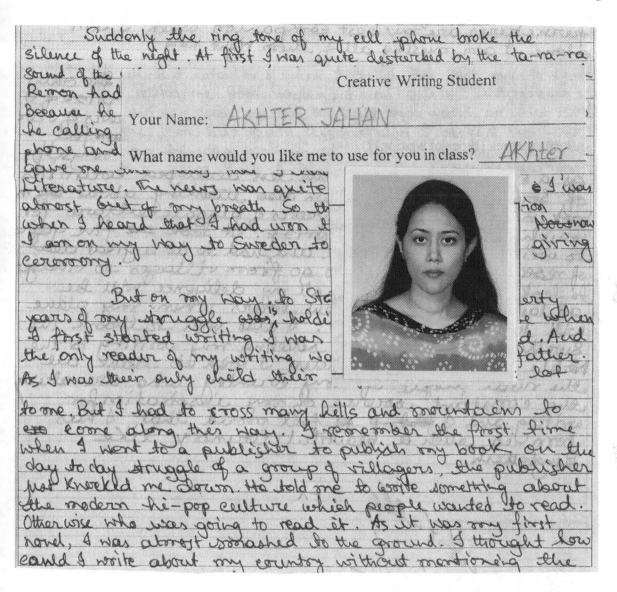

Suddenly the ring tone of my cell phone broke the
silence of the night. At first I was quite disturbed by the ta-ra-ra
sound of the
Remon had
Because he
he calling
phone and
gave me
Literature. The news was quite
almost out of my breath. So th
when I heard that I had won
I am on my way to Sweden to
ceremony.

Creative Writing Student

Your Name: AKHTER JAHAN

What name would you like me to use for you in class? Akhter

I was

Nowshow

giving

erty

when

d. And

father.

lot

But on my way to Sto
years of my struggle was holdi
I first started writing I was
the only reader of my writing wa
As I was their only child their

to me. But I had to cross many hills and mountains to
come along this way. I remember the first time
when I went to a publisher to publish my book on the
day to day struggle of a group of villagers, the publisher
just kneeled me down. He told me to write something about
the modern hi-pop culture which people wanted to read.
Otherwise who was going to read it. As it was my first
novel, I was almost smashed to the ground. I thought how
could I write about my country without mentioning the

Nasrin Akter

Ladies and gentleman, honourable guests, my dear
writers. I am very glad to present here in this very
shining _____ my
feelings _____ thank you
very much _____ ed me
to be _____

I am m _____ honourable
award in the world for the _____ based
on social life of my country _____ know
the name of my book "R _____ deshi
people. I was wrote abou _____ y spend
their time, how they survive _____

But I never even in drea _____ Nobel
prize even not in dream. O _____ told me
that your book is selected _____ the
nomination of Nobel prize _____ ieve it
_____ wants _____ But
_____ me I was surprised. Though when
I _____ to torture mentally when I
_____ about the subject. For writing
_____ stay with them and observe
_____ for many days I lived in
_____ time some _____ of my relatives
_____ ave this. For the writing I have to
_____ from my family. So, many had
_____ because my husband didn't understa

Creative Writing Student

Your Name: _Nasrin Akter_

What name would you like me to use for you in class? _Dri_

Picture:

Shaima Laskar

Short Story:
Mina & Rina: An Allegorical Tale

Winning The Nobel Prize was A Wonderful Experience

Dear ladees … I gentleman thanks a lot for being here with me to
acheive this
wonderful a
that made my d
the city or
making my d
a child. On the BBC news when I s
won the nobel I wondered and hoped t
to win the world's most prestigious
prize. Since I was I child I liked to r
short stories. At the age of 10 I w
300 hundred short stories and twelve n
and poems nobody could beleeve that
At the age of 15 I fell in love wit
are John Keats, Gerard Manley Hopkin
W.B Yeats and last but not the least
Emily   Elizabeth Bishop

Creative Writing Student

Your Name: Shaima Laskar

What name would you like me to use for you in class? Shaima

there
ly Nobel
els and
poems,
stories
a it.
s. The
and
ad
I

Rea   Poems I felt that I was in love with them
and   and there tragedy poems or novels I felt that
I w   moment and it really hurted me. Because
I w   in literature my father decided for me to
sta   rature. I was very happy to study in my
knew   ile I was a student some students thought
tr   ck on my head because I was so involved
in   lories that made others think that I'm a
liti   my university life I fell in love with my
Dr   fessor Allan. S. Frost. I could share all my
em   with him. After a few months he also

Nur Bahar Alif

Creative Writing Student

Your Name: Nur Bahar Alif

What name would you like me to use for you in class? Nur

Idrak Hossain

Autobiography, Biography & Memoir:
Memoir
Why?

Poetry:
Falsely Mesmerize
The End
Wild Horses
Obscured
Prometheus Unbound
Drifting Away
A Relic of My Past

Short Story:
10 Minutes in a Bar

Drama:
Warfield

Creative Writing Student

Your Name: Idrak Hossain

What name would you like me to use for you in class? Idrak

I, being a humble ma... indeed to recieve this in front of such a respected and acknowle... I would request them t... any lacks in my ... ary already I... group of people.

...onoured ...us award ...iversally ...ple. Excuse ...me for ...my legs ...s this

I, being a resident ... third world ...ountry grew up seein... ...ave see some ...eople driving Mazda on ...road and others starving to death and begging for a single ...oin to survive the day on the otherside of the ...oad. I have seen corruption to the full and ...ave observed it well to figure out the reasons ...ehind it. I have seen ...generation and faced a generation gap between me, as a teenager ...owing up in the era of internet and sattelite ...elevision and my parents, who as a teenager ...d the slightest idea of television and

VI

Kazi Sarmad Karim

Poetry:
Memoirs of a Realization
Three Haikus
Seven Epigrams

Short Story:
Belonging

As I cleared my throat uncomfortably, I definetly felt

Creative Writing Student

Your Name: ___Kazi Sarmad Karim___

What name would you like me to use for you in class? ___Sarmad___

What had hap... well he had
gone on stage comfort... en the podium
with composure and t... The whole world
was looking, his family, ...ell-wishers and
he coughed! For a m... nutie . the
world stopped, not ...ed or created
a sound.
Then he sort... nposure and
said, "... It fels g... ...rst person
... ever to start ... a cough."
And the ... ...om seemed
to ebb away. Some people laughed, some chuckled
while others smiled.
He continued "Your Highness, esteemed
...tleman and those
Good Evening".
... a tightness somewhere
..., I was able to sidestep
...bered Erfan saying
...se you'll jumble it
...and simple and add
...mumbo-jumbo. 'Cuz you

Alipha Khan

Poetry:
Poem based on a self-created Metaphor
Poem connecting the words: Joy, Cook, and Outer Space
Thoughts
Found, lost . . . . .
Untitled
)eath becomes Her
Title-less
Freud's Field Day
Shadow Puppet

Short Story:
Excerpt from a Prankster's Portfolio

it is, the day she's been waiting for.

Creative Writing Student

Alipha Khan

such dream What name would you like me to use for you in class? Alipha

actor, art.... forth with the longing of one ac child it is so easy to be someo else the next. If only it was th

Picture: ....er, ...
someone

Like her peers, Alipha wanted to girl. Then came the appalling realisa non-existence of Santa Clause: he v ly le self-

e as a little
as the
nly choose
er life to
ppiness
riting and

middle rows, an all-knowing his lips. He has been with nfused and confusing adolescence, she lost her parents and tedly rejected, her thirties clutches of a nervous breakdown ed - still standing, and a little niser. They were the best of , and he couldn't help feeling

Mahreen Murad

Autobiography, Biography & Memoir:
Nana
Encounter with the Prune

Poetry:
How do I hate thee?

In anticipation, the hall grew quiet. Some people at the back get her the eyes red

She walked toward smiled before she spoke
distinctly heard th
thought then sh

"When I was a child
women and hence I
were created from one
I was as far bac
resented this and wh
how men think they pos
them, 'their' women
rib".

ing Her) i
s and
about how
Man's)
. Since
ember, i
. more is
around
he single

more breaths. Maybe
held a little away.
every member of the
in the front row,
e them and at me.
to gauge their reactions
e continuing.

Creative Writing Student

Your Name: Mahreen Murad

What name would you like me to use for you in class? Mahreen

Picture:

Nadia Nusrat

Dear Honourable Ladies & Gentlemen,

a very good evening to all of you. First of all, I want to thank everybody who have helped me to get this _____ to thank my

_____ want to have
_____ giving
me th _____ that
you the Nobel prize for _____ welfare works.
I am not only happy for t _____ ve I got. I
am also feeling glad that I _____ ing for human
beings something for world _____ tress people
My works is Social Welf _____ a very little

Creative Writing Student

Your Name: _Nadia Nusrat_

What name would you like me to use for you in class? _Nusrat_

Picture:

age _____ elp peop _____ ed to survive
peo _____ iseries _____ o do it practically
I g _____ ion giv _____ ather Teresa. Sh
is _____ hen I first saw her in Television. I
her _____ her helping nature. From that day, I h
fol _____ arted my work from my school life
Whe _____ versity & started helping people
in _____ in the middle of my education I wen

Bushra Rahman

Your Majesty, the king, Ladies and gentleman, and the ministers., The Noble prize committee.

a very

First

as you

I am very glad that
me for this prize this y
respect for me.

Your majestry, the prize
f from 1901. Literature
sectors of this. I was a
30 years back.
from when I was 12 y
in my dream I was
nobel prize but not
tried to improve my wri

people.
their psychological
pact on society.
started focusing on
for which I have
ize has the same

re, as we know the
society, as it reflects

Creative Writing Student

Your Name: _Bushra Rahman_

What name would you like me to use for you in class? _Bushra_

Picture:

great

issen

iteratere

iting

the

lways

+ dimention

like

S. M. Walid Rahman

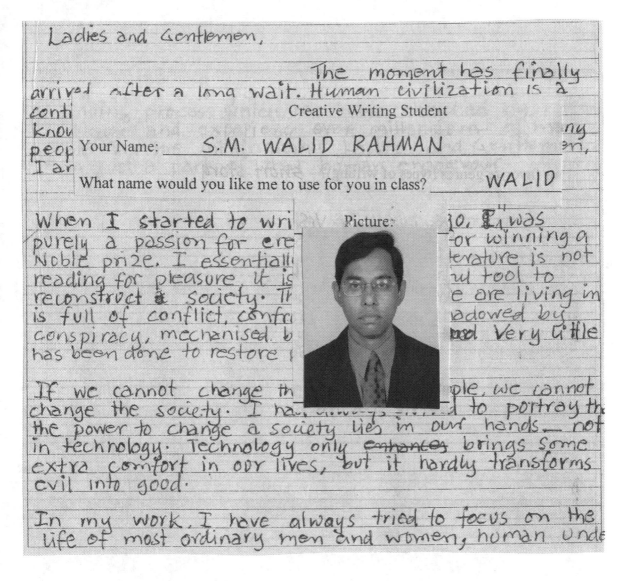

Ladies and Gentlemen,

The moment has finally arrived after a long wait. Human civilization is a conti... Creative Writing Student know... peop... I an...

Your Name: S.M. WALID RAHMAN

What name would you like me to use for you in class? WALID

When I started to wri... Picture: ...jo, I was purely a passion for cre... ...or winning a Noble prize. I essentiall... ...erature is not reading for pleasure, it is ...ul tool to reconstruct a society. Th... ...e are living in is full of conflict, confr... ...adowed by conspiracy, mechanised. b... ...and very little has been done to restore ...

If we cannot change th... ...ple, we cannot change the society. I hav... ...ed to portray th... the power to change a society lies in our hands — not in technology. Technology only ~~enhances~~ brings some extra comfort in our lives, but it hardly transforms evil into good.

In my work, I have always tried to focus on the life of most ordinary men and women, human unde...

Hildibrand Sarker

Creative Writing Student

Your Name: HILDIBRAND SARKER

What name would you like me to use for you in class? HILDI

Sameeha Suraiya

Autobiography, Biography & Memoir:
On a Hot Summer's Day

Poetry:
A Station at Night
Catastrophe

Short Story:
Caged for Life

The dawn gave birth to a new day — the day that had been awaited by millions around the ~~an~~ that were Januar~~y~~ prize, ~~to~~ in tune ~~with the various~~

The event began ~~in~~ Hall. Dignitaries from all ~~the~~ spheres of life started ~~to~~ the young and the old, the successful, they were peop~~le~~ colours — this event broug~~ht~~ the hearts beating as one, the great doors and the

The audience ~~was~~ corners of the globe. It was would want to be a part politicians to press, the place buzzed with a flurry of excitement.

One by one, the nobel prizes were announced and given — it was a bitter sweet moment. Lives were changed, some winners broke down. For some, however, it was just a moment of dignified silence, the respect that was gained after years of sheer determination and hard work

Creative Writing Student

Your Name: Sameeha Suraiya

What name would you like me to use for you in class? Sameeha

XV

Parsa Tazsrian

Creative Writing Student

Your Name: Parsa Tazsrian

What name would you like me to use for you in class? Parsa

(for literature.)

"Good evening ladies and gentlemen. I'm honoured to receive

a special
ceremony
I would return with the
thought, I would act this
"I remember that
publishing my first book. D
me down. But I still we
to publish my first book
"My book became
children. The film-makers
on it. The children could n
to be published. It was sold
Potter movies were box-
for children. Infact I was
children.
"The children are more creative than we are.
Often we see children having imaginary friends. They
speak to their imaginary friends and talk to them.
Once I went to a park for picnik with my friends.
There I saw a child picking up a dirty stick while
playing with his friends. He was pretending to be a
magician.

Do not say, "It is morning," and dismiss it with a name of yesterday. See it for the first time as a newborn child that has no name.

--

Rabindranth Tagore

Experiment in Creativity: A special English Writing Course in Bangladesh

[First published in the *Himeji JALT Journal, Volume 9. No. 1, pp. 1 – 2.*]

By Dr. Patrick Dougherty

The desire to write grows with writing.
–Erasmus

From March 3 – April 4th, 2006, I had the privilege of being a volunteer visiting professor at Presidency University, in Dhaka, Bangladesh. While there, I taught an experimental class to a group of EFL students and educators, and many occasional observers. The topic, and a subject of a study I am conducting, was and is *Creative Writing as a Motivational Resource in EFL/ESL*. The official title of the class I taught was Creative Writing in English, but it quickly became known among my students as Dr. Pat's Writing Class. Below are the official course description and the statement of goals as given to the students. They quickly give an idea of all that was expected of my at-first, shell-shocked students.

COURSE DESCRIPTION
Creative Writing in English will provide an opportunity for students to hone their creative writing skills as well as provide a student-centered environment for English language immersion.   Students will explore and develop their own ideas through the medium of creative writing. Students will read, write, and share their creative endeavors and providing constructive advice to their peers. The participants in the course will become a small community of writers, eager to compose, share, read, hear, and support.

COURSE GOALS
 Students will learn and practice skills that help them craft unique and thoughtful work in English. They will sharpen their critical reading skills through reading, discussion, and writing assignments and will learn the conventions of critique and collaboration. They will maintain a portfolio of revised work and they will submit selected pieces of their creative work to a course literary book.

Once the shock wore off, they got busy engaging in a rare opportunity. Creative writing courses in even the native language are rare in Bangladesh. As one of my students wrote in a final essay she submitted, "In [Bangladesh] there are not enough opportunities to do such a course as we have done with Dr. Dougherty. So it was quite an unusual event for the students who successfully completed the course."
        Creative writing in English is normally not considered the domain of the EFL or ESL student, but rather, as the prerogative of the native speaker. The class that I taught demonstrated that introducing creative writing to ESL or EFL programs can serve as a powerful motivational force in the classroom, benefiting the students academically, emotionally, and linguistically.
        There were fifteen students. They ranged in age from sixteen years old to approximately forty years old. Fourteen of them were attending the class for a

grade and one was attending as an audit. There were four men and eleven women. Most were university students from one of three universities in Dhaka, Bangladesh: Presidency University (which sponsored the class), North South University, and Dhaka University. One of the students was a high school student, and several of the students were university graduates either working full or part-time jobs. We met four times per week over the four-week period, with each class lasting two hours. During that time my students were thrown into the caldron of their own creativity. What they produced over such a short period of time was quite remarkable. During that manic and fruitful time-frame they each successfully completed a biographical sketch or a memoir, at least forty lines of poetry, a short story, and, in teams of four or five students, a play. The students who had the unique opportunities of being writers, actors, directors, and stage designers put the plays that they created into production. The students even found the time to put on (with my gentle encouragement) two poetry and short story reading sessions for local educators and media personalities.

I will be returning to Bangladesh to continue the class series and my study over the course of the next two years. I am working with Bangladeshi educators to follow the students' progress and to answer the all-important questions of whether they are still writing and whether the opportunity to use English in a creative manner has motivated them to new heights of language acquisition. I have been gathering my research data via focus groups and student questionnaires. My preliminary findings will be given in a paper that I am scheduled to deliver to at the AsiaTEFL conference in Fukuoka on August 20th, 2006. Shedding the jargon of applied linguistics and TEFL for a moment, I will simply say that I saw light in my student's eyes, a strong desire to tell their own stories using the English medium, and an enthusiastic response to the challenge of writing creatively. Aside from my study objectives, one of my goals with the class was to, as I said in my course outline, *"collect enough brilliant examples of student creative work to make a course literary booklet to serve as a permanent reminder for the students of the experience of taking the course and to exhibit their talent to the wider community."* The book will be titled <u>Deshi Dreams</u> and it will be published at the end of the summer.

Dr. Patrick Dougherty works in the Global Communication Department of the University of Hyogo, Himeji, Japan, and he may be reached at this e-mail address: pdougherty@shse.u-hyogo.ac.jp

Acknowledgements

It was my great privilege to travel to Bangladesh to conduct the first of a series of special courses on creative writing. It was an experience that was satisfying to me on many levels: professionally, in my research, and most importantly, as a teacher.

Many people helped in making the course a reality. I would like to express my special thanks to the following individuals who gave such support that the course would not have been possible without them.

Dr. Arifa Rahman, for organizing the class, gathering an excellent group of student writers, and providing assistance and counsel through the duration of the course.

Professor Dr. Harunur Rashid, Pro Vice Chancellor of Presidency University for hosting the course and providing me with logistic support and housing.

Finally, I would like to express my thanks to my students. You were brave, you were interesting, and you were a joy to work with. Thank you for your perseverance, faith, senses of humor, and wonderful creativity.

With kind regards,

Pat

Dr. Patrick T. Dougherty
Department of Global Communication
University of Hyogo
Himeji, Japan

OVERTURE:
ON TEACHING

Patrick Dougherty

You forever feel
immured
transfixed
to the shore

Its mystical in doses
harsh and brittle in pieces
like cuts of glass falling
through water by degrees

Like a builder of ships
you saw
cut
weld
hammer
tear apart
rebuild
curse and sweat

Then all you can do
is stand on the shore and wave
as the creations wrought from your toil
slip their coils
take sail
and disappear

Contents:

The book is arranged to follow the plan of the course. It is organized in four sections according to the genres that were introduced, and in the order that they were introduced. We delved into four areas of literature: biography, autobiography, and memoir; poetry; short story; and, finally, drama. After the drama section there is a special section where you can meet the writers from the Creative Writing Class. Last, there is an appendix where the course syllabus is provided.

Autobiography, Biography & Memoir		**Page 2**
Golden Delight	Akhter Jahan	Page 3
Nana	Mahreen Murad	Page 5
Memoir	Idrak Hossain	Page 7
Changes in Life	Parsa Tazrian	Page 8
On a Hot Summer's Day	Sameeha Suraiya	Page 14
Encounter with the Prune	Mahreen Murad	Page 15
Why?	Idrak Hossain	Page 17

Poetry		**Page 19**
A Station at Night	Sameeha Suraiya	Page 20
Catastrophe	Sameeha Suraiya	Page 20
I have no Idea	Nasrin Akter	Page 20
A Poem: Moi	Kashfi Ahmed	Page 21
A Poem of Myself	Nur Bahar Alif	Page 22
Poem Based on . . .	Alipha Khan	Page 23
Poem Connecting . . .	Alipha Khan	Page 24
Thoughts	Alipha Khan	Page 24
Found, Lost . . .	Alipha Khan	Page 24
Untitled	Alipha Khan	Page 25
Death Becomes Her	Alipha Khan	Page 25
Title-less	Alipha Khan	Page 26
Freud's Field Day	Alipha Khan	Page 26
Shadow Puppet	Alipha Khan	Page 26
Falsely Mesmerize	Idrak Hossain	Page 27
The End	Idrak Hossain	Page 27
Wild Horses	Idrak Hossain	Page 28
Obscured	Idrak Hossain	Page 28
Prometheus Unbound	Idrak Hossain	Page 28
Drifting Away	Idrak Hossain	Page 28
A Relic of my Past	Idrak Hossain	Page 29
Three Haikus	Kazi Sarmad Karim	Page 29
Memoirs of a Realization	Karzi Sarmad Karim	Page 29
Seven Epigrams	Karzi Sarmad Karim	Page 30
How do I hate thee?	Mahreen Murad	Page 30
The Inevitable Truth	Bushra Rahman	Page 31

Short Story   **Page 33**
Belonging   Kazi Sarmad Karim   Page 34
An Honest Shepard . . .   Nur Bahar Alif   Page 36
Mina & Rina . . .   Shaima Laskar   Page 39
Caged for Life   Sameeha Suraiya   Page 41
Excerpt . . .   Alipha Khan   Page 42
10 Minutes in a Bar   Idrak Hossain   Page 44
Whispered Recall   Hildibrand Sarker   Page 54

Drama   **Page 60**
War field   Idrak Hossain   Page 61

Meet the Writers   **Page 69**
Class Snapshots   Page I
Kashfi Ahmed   Page II
Akhter Jahan   Page III
Nasrin Akter   Page IV
Nur Bahar Alif   Page V
Idrak Hossain   Page VI
Kazi Sarmad Karim   Page VII
Alipha Khan   Page VIII
Shaima Laskar   Page IX
Mahreen Murad   Page X
Nadia Nusrat   Page XI
Bushra Rahman   Page XII
S. M. Walid Rahman   Page XIII
Hildibrand Sarker   Page XIV
Sameeha Suraiya   Page XV
Parsa Tazsrian   Page XVI

Appendix: **The Creative Writing in English Course Syllabus**

Quiz: Why do you want to write creatively?

Adapted from Rozakis, the <u>C. I. Guide to Creative Writing</u>, 2004
[Given the first day of class]

I want to write creatively because . . .

1. ___ I want to learn more about myself.
2. ___ I want to learn more about the world.
3. ___ I need to heal old wounds.
4. ___ I have a story I want to hand down through the ages.
5. ___ I have information to share.
6. ___ I want to entertain people with the power of my pen.
7. ___ I want to make the world a better place.
8. ___ I want to fulfill a dream.

This is my letter to the World
That never wrote to Me —
The simple News that Nature told —
With tender Majesty

Her Message is committed
To Hands I cannot see —
For love of Her — Sweet countrymen —
Judge tenderly — of Me

Emily Dickinson (1830 – 1886)

THE FIRST WEEK:
AUTOBIOGRAPHY, BIOGRAPHY & MEMOIR:

Grownups love figures. When you tell them that you have made a new friend, they never ask you any questions about essential matters. They never say to you, "What does his voice sound like? What games does he love best? Does he collect butterflies?" Instead they demand: "How old is he? How many brothers has he? How much does he weigh? How much money does his father make?" Only from these figures do they think they have learned anything about him. -- Antoine de Saint-Exupery, <u>The Little Prince</u>

Autobiography:

Use the characterization sheet for each of the possibilities below:

❖ Locate one "action" event in your life that answers the question: *Who am I?*

❖ Write in the third person. *Maybe even through the eyes and thoughts of a non-human – your pet, perhaps.*

❖ Describe yourself as you were when you were eight years old – *in the voice of yourself when you were eight. What was your life like? What was/is life like for a Bangladeshi eight-year old?*

Biography:

❖ Interview of a Peer/A Friend: *Use the characterization sheet and then choose something about his or her day that will explain him or her to me, allowing me to understand who this person really is. OPTION: Describe this person as he or she was at the age of eight – in his or her voice as an eight year old. What was life like?*

❖ Grandparent Interview: *Use the characterization sheet and the grandparent interview sheet.*

❖ A teacher or instructor interview: *Use the characterization sheet and the teacher interview questions or make your own.*

Memoir:

❖ Focus on a significant event in your life (good or bad) – *introduce us to you by recounting it and your reaction.*

❖ Take an intense event from your life and write a description of it in great detail: *It can be a wedding, a funeral, a class experience, a vacation, a journey, anything, but it should be something intense and interesting to you. You may use the five senses descriptive sheet to help you organize your writing.*

Golden Delight
Akhter Jahan

Hello everyone! I am Akhter from Bangladesh. I wanted to share some wonderful experiences with you about how my theoretical experience of reading literature turned into practice while I was doing a creative writing course in English. I think you will enjoy it. In our country there are not enough opportunities to do such a course as we have done with Dr. Dougherty. So it was quite an unusual event for the students who successfully completed the course.

When my teachers, Dr. Arifa Rahman and Dr. Rubina Khan, first told me about the course, it seemed quite interesting to me. And my interest was enhanced when I heard that Dr. Pat would conduct the course. I had the chance to know him as a resource person when I worked as a volunteer for BELTA (Bangladesh English Language Teachers Association) during their Teacher Training Program in March 25 – 30, 2005. So, I decided to do the course without having any idea of the course content. But after having signed up, when I first got in touch with the content, I shivered with excitement, wonder, fear and did not know what else. Because the course content said that the students had to write an autobiography, biography, memoir, haiku, poem, short story, and drama by themselves in the class and only in one month. So the task seemed quite impossible to me. But I took it as a challenge and thought, "Let's see what happens."

Our classes started on March 3, 2006 and finished April 4, 2006. From this adventure I got assets that will help me for the rest of my life. Not only me but also many of my classmates could hardly imagine that we could write down any literary pieces. But Dr. Pat made it possible for us with his warm and constant inspiration and patient support. He brought us out from the darkness of night to the brightness of daylight and made us believe that we have the ability to express our thoughts in writing. Thanks, Dr. Pat for coming all the way from Japan to teach us here at Presidency University.

The most alarming moment in our class arrived when Dr. Pat said that we had to write down at least forty lines of poetry. Almost all of us except one or two had ever done this type of task before. So we were shocked and my reaction was, "Okay, I am done with the course and this will definitely be my last class!" But, quite surprisingly, I attended the next class because of the way our teacher encouraged us and explained in the class about writing poetry. The task became easier for us and, indeed, a bit exciting. My excitement reached a peak when I sat down and my pen started moving on the paper and, thus, my first poem came to life.

The most enjoyable part of our course was the drama section where the students were divided into four groups, each containing four or five students. Each group had to come up with its own production on the stage. This task was quite exciting and challenging for us. Besides, through this assignment all of my classmates starting from Kashfi, a tenth grade student, to Walid who had been teaching at an English medium school for the last eleven years, became intimate friends. We performed dramas called *Warfield, Kindergarten Kids,* and also on some family themes and thus got one more chance to discover ourselves.

So, Dr. Pat, I am inviting you on behalf of all my classmates that you would again come to Bangladesh in the future and would give us, along with new students, another wonderful opportunity to raise our self confidence higher and would also help us to discover ourselves through literature.

Nana
Mahreen Murad

He wakes up at eight every morning and gets cranky. His eyes don't see that well since the stroke six months ago and he can't read the small print of the newspaper anymore. A bellow gets someone to rush in and read the paper – a misplaced stress and he makes a face, "That'll do," he says and dismisses the reader, always a perfectionist. He does not realize he says *probhoke* instead of *provoke* but when he hears someone else say it wrong, he is quick to point it out – innocently, without seeming to think it rude. Another bellow. Another reader. Another dismissal.

Bellow after bellow until he wakes up the person he had wanted in the first place. While he listens to the news being read out by her, she carefully lifts his hands and submerges them in a curious bowl of soapy water, to soften the nails. He concentrates on all the words being read and immediately shoots a quizzical look at her, his seventeen-year old granddaughter, when insignificant paragraphs are skipped to make the process quicker; he notices the gaps in meaning and grunts at being underestimated.

This morning newspaper reading session is his favorite game now and a challenge too; every challenge has always been taken seriously. The nail cutting session will follow the reading session today, the first Friday of every month. She has already laid out all the necessary instruments beside him for his inspection. He takes his hands out of the water and holds them up so they drip all over her, for she has to sit very close as he does not hear too well, until she takes the towel and dries them off delicately.

His nails become soft from the soapy water but they are thick and difficult to clip with the prehistoric nail cutter he insists on using. It takes half an hour just to get rid of the nails and then another half an hour to file them into shape. Once they are done, he softly sweeps his nails over the top of his upper lip to see if they are done smoothly but they are never done properly enough to satisfy him and they need to be re-filed at regular intervals several times the day that they are cut.

The clenching and unclenching of his hands show how he is concerned about something. He is very perturbed at the death of his pigeons. Every afternoon he carefully places two handfuls of birdseed on the windowsill and steps back to the divan in the living room to watch the birds. The pigeons know their elderly crony and squawk at him from the bars of the grill. From his dancing eyes she can tell that he gets great pleasure from his noisy pigeons that dirty the windowsill that he insists on being washed and cleaned every night when the birds are away.

The guard comes in at nine thirty, as ordered at half hour intervals, to announce the number of his pet pigeons since they have been dying of some disease and this time the number is one less that it had been at the last count half an hour ago. The reason – a cat ate a bird.

As in natural agreement, heavy footsteps are heard trying to be faster. A wrinkled forehead made wrinklier by the frown of frustration at his body's betrayal, moves toward the display cabinet to grab the shotgun that has not been used for years but is cleaned and polished. The slow body moves determinedly to the open balcony of the second floor.

The cat can be seen licking itself on the wall. He takes aim, carefully, squinting very hard, trying to see – his left arm shakes from the effort at holding up the barrel of the gun and his left eye is closed. A deafening shot is heard; the cat falls off the wall . . . surprisingly accurate.

He walks back to his bed confidently, chest out; the walk has a hint of a swagger and his triumph lights up his ancient eyes that give little away but tears when he talks about his mother in the dead of the night after he wakes up from a disturbing dream; even the left one with which he does not see at all. When teased about the walk, only a coy smile appears on a once handsome face that used to get many, many smiles from pretty girls in his youth.

Memoir
Idrak Hossain

The grey clouds didn't allow even the strongest darting rays of the sun to enter. On a weekend like that who would want to get up early in the morning? No one, I guessed. But luck, or rather bad luck compelled me and fourteen other students to get up early on that morning and head towards a tutor's house.

Like other days, I woke up late and was sure to reach my tutor's house tardy. I woke up, got ready, skipped breakfast and hit the road with a rickshaw. Even then I hadn't the slimmest idea of what the day was to add to my experience. I was having a glimpse every now and then at my wristwatch, anxiously, to see whether I would make it to my tutor's house on time and make him and all the others wonder "What went wrong today – he is on time?" or I'd reach the house late as usual and get the usual scolding?

"I am still an eighth grader. What will happen to me when I pass university and start working at a job? I hate waking up early in the morning," thought I. Weird thoughts were flashing through my eighth grade mind. I had another glance at my wristwatch and said to myself, "Nice, according to my calculations, I'll be just 10 minutes late. I am gradually improving."

I was almost there and was almost sure that I'd be at maximum ten minutes late. I still hadn't the slimmest idea of what the day would force me to witness, something which I never wanted but something that will never be wiped from my memory.

There was a bus stand near my tutor's house and for some reason an old man there stole my attention. It was probably because I saw him missing the bus, either because age had made him a "slow couch" or because of the heavy bag he was carrying or maybe because of both. Near the bus stand there was always a traffic jam and getting stuck there enabled me to capture those morning rush hour sights everyday. The old man missed a *Mirpur-Dhanmondi* bus and was waiting for another one. Suddenly, a speeding bus hit him from the back and I saw him thrown a few feet in the air and his black-framed spectacles and his huge bag tossed away.

Maybe it was his age that kept him from moving out of the way quickly, like the others. The old man was moaning loudly and was crying out for people and God's help. The speeding bus quickly fled from the scene without picking up anyone. I saw the crowd gather around him, and the words of that old man still ring in my ears. Sitting on the rickshaw put me above the crowd and gave a clear view of the dying old man. I saw fresh dark blood gushing out from the back of his head. The scene was so terrible that it was better to see someone cutting off his own leg to save his family in the movie "Saw." At least that wasn't real. The sight of the blood and his utterances left me numb. I moved not a single millimeter or heard anything but his moaning. I was staring straight, almost unwillingly, at that sight. I came back from my trance when I felt water on my head. It was raining.

Changes in Life
Parsa Tazrian

Me:	*Ma, why are we leaving?*
Mother:	*Dear, I got a better job there. We are leaving next week. So pack up your things, I'll help you with that in a few minutes.*
Me:	*But what about my friends? I don't know anyone there. What am I gonna do there?*
Mother:	*Oh, you'll make new friends there. And we have all our relatives there. Moreover you dad's there, too. You are going to like that place.*
Me:	*What about Tabby and Spotty? They are very sensitive. They don't come to anyone else except me. What are they gonna do without me?"*
Mother:	*They'll be with your cousins . . . Now go, go, go, go!"*
Me:	*But Ma!!*
Mother:	*Now what?*
Me:	*Did you ask Rubab? Does he wanna go? Why are you taking us?*
Mother:	*He's still very young to understand all this. So he will go wherever I tell him to go. He's not a naughty kid like you.*
Me:	*I'm naughty? Where? How?*
Mother:	*Are you a good girl? If so, go to your room and start packing you and your brother's clothes.*
Me:	*What? But Ma!!!!!*
Mother:	*No more ifs and buts, young lady.*

With that, Mother pushed me out of the room. I did not know what to do; I really did not want to go back to Bangladesh. I heard it was a creepy place. Mother got a good job offer in Canada when I was about four years old, and my brother was hardly two years old. But Father was working in Bangladesh as a popular professor at Dhaka University (the best university in Bangladesh). Dhaka University was known as the Oxford of the east. Anyway, since then we had stayed in Ottawa, the capital of Canada, with our grandparents. We had many relatives living close by. There I started my schooling from kindergarten. I was really fond of pets; so, on my 6th birthday, my cousins gave me two Siamese cats. We later decided to call them Tabby and Spotty. When I was in grade six, Mother gave us the shock of our lives. She wanted to return to Bangladesh, as she had gotten a better job offer there. We never thought that we would have to leave the place where we grew up and go to an unknown place. We were already adapted to the culture and environment there, in Canada. We did not know the Bengali language; nor did we have any idea of the kind of people living there, their culture, their mentality, or anything.

By the following week we were in Bangladesh, leaving everyone and everything in Canada. We landed in Dhaka, the capital. The airport was not as big as the one back in Canada. As soon as we got out of the arrivals area and out to the car I noticed how hot it was, but the heat was not as irritating as the beggars begging for money. Then there was the traffic jam, the car horns, everyone talking in a different language – it all was quite unbearable. I thought that I would be able to just take a shower and go to sleep when I reached my new home. But that was not to be. As soon as we got to the house people -- many, many, people, greeted us. People we had not seen for ages, people I did not know, the house was full of people. Resting, which was what I really wanted to do, was out of the question. Instead, I had entered Relative Hell. Someone had prepared food for us; others were greeting us. It seemed as if the house belonged to someone else and we were the ones visiting. Instead of resting, my brother and I had to sit with all the people and talk very formally with them. I felt like pushing all the people out of the house. Instead of that we had to sit down to a heavy meal. The food was so rich that I could hardly digest it. I suffered from a stomachache for a week. My brother suffered the same.

Me: *God! It was way beyond all my horrible expectations. Utterly unbearable!*

I wanted to leave the place as soon as possible, and that was impossible. There was no escape from circumstances; we were already trapped in that house, in that country, in that situation. My first day in Bangladesh was terrible. I think back to that day and am practically speechless; it still freaks me out. When I was having a stomach problem, our neighbors and relatives came by with many herbal remedies. I was forced to drink some disgusting concoctions. After all of this suffering, I stopped talking to my parents for a while. Mother started going to her workplace the following week. My brother and I were trying to adjust to the new environment when we got what we thought was good news. My father said that we would start school the next month. I could not wait to go to school. I loved my school back in Canada. It had been really huge, full of students and nice teachers. It had been really fun. I thought the schools in Bangladesh would be the same. I could not wait to go to school. But the day I went to school was also a day of big disappointments. We had to wear uniforms. The teachers were not so nice. The school was not so big. When I entered the school for the first time, I felt like everyone was staring at me. I did not want to go there again. I first went to meet my new class-teacher. She was the head teacher in charge of my class. She was a very pretty lady. But she was not as nice as she looked. Back in Canada the teachers were friendly. Here my teacher did not talk to me nicely or give me even a smile. Instead she looked at me with keen eyes.

Teacher: *You missed a few classes. Meet me during the lunchtime break and I'll update you on all the recent happenings, the homework, the coming tests, and upcoming events.*

Me: *Yes, Ma'am.*

Teacher: *[In a stern voice] Now what are you doing here? The assembly is going to start any minute.*

I went to attend the assembly. All the students were singing the national anthem of Bangladesh. I felt really left out. Maybe some students noticed that I was standing quietly in the line instead of singing. After the assembly was over and we were on our way to class, one girl was very friendly and asked me if I was new in town. We did not get much time to talk as we entered the classroom and a teacher came in to take attendance. After that another teacher came in and started the class. That class ended, the teacher left and another teacher came in to begin another class. This continued for three more lessons. In between we got no recesses, no real breaks. We had to take continual dictation, sitting quietly at our desks. Finally, we did have a break, a half-hour for lunch. My class-teacher ate up that time updating me on all the homework and materials that I had missed.

The teachers gave us loads of homework. The school was horrible; the teachers were monsters. The first few days I made up a lot of excuses not to attend school. Soon I was out of excuses. Finally, I decided to attend classes regularly. I tried to get into the environment. I made new friends at school, and got used to taking all the pressure in a few months. Then came our final exams. The exams lasted for one week. Two weeks later we got our report cards, and I was satisfied with my results. About that time, I found out that Bangladeshi people could be very narrow-minded. And it hurt.

We had a class party before the school closed for a holiday. We were told that we did not need to wear the school uniform that day, but could come in "casual clothes." I went to the party wearing a short-skirt and a tight top, which was what I considered to be casual clothes. At least it would have been an acceptable casual outfit in Canada. Not so in Bangladesh. When I entered class I noticed that all the girls were wearing *kameezes*, and everyone was staring at me. For a while it seemed that they had never seen a girl before. Afterwards, the party got going and everything seemed fine.

School reopened, and I went back to school. Everyone was giving me a weird look. Some people even started calling me a very irritating name. My friends were quite annoyed with me. No one was ready to explain to me what was happening; rather they were having fun at my expense. I started getting prank calls at home. Never did I think that things that were so accepted in Canada would be considered strange in Bangladesh. What made matters worse was that our neighbors found out about this, and they started gossiping about it rather than helping us or standing by me. Someone even said that if a few more children started acting like me than the future of society would be dark. I had always thought of myself as a good girl, just a regular kid. Things got bad, so bad that my mother got angry with me one day and even hit me. I guess she felt a great deal of pressure from those around her. If I was in Canada, I thought, I could just sue everyone. But I wasn't in Canada, and I had no one who was willing to listen to me or help me out. Everyone considered the incident to be my fault. I stopped going to school for a couple of months. Finally one day a friend of mine called up.

Friend: *Be a brave girl. Face the situation strongly. If you keep on*
                    missing classes you will fail, and everyone will say that you
                    deserve it because you are guilty. They will be happy. Fight them,
                    join class as soon as possible and get back to work.

These words gave me lots of strength, and I was confident that I could easily face the devastating situation. My friend stood by me from that moment onwards. She proved herself. She was a friend in word and in deed. With her support, I started my classes again. Soon I was able to cope with the pressure; I knew I could survive in the class. Even so, I missed Canada. There, people just accepted and appreciated me for who I was. Over here people had gotten it into their minds that I was a bad person, they did not look at me in any other way. It was black and white to them. They would not give me a chance to show them who I really was. It was hard, but my friends at school made life bearable. I was able to go on.

Interestingly, I soon noticed a trend followed by the students at my school. The girls hardly talked to the boys and considered even sitting by them to be a great crime. I thought of changing that trend. I started openly talking to the boys, and making friends with them. Following my example, other girls started to treat the boys as friends.

It was one of my friend's birthdays (and he was a boy). We decided to give him a surprise party. The day before the party everyone was talking over the phone to one another, almost continuously, as we planned for the party. I was getting many calls from my friends, some of whom were boys. My parents did not really like the fact that I was getting calls from boys, but they ignored it. When I asked my parents for permission to go to the party, they made the whole thing into a big issue. Back in Canada, no one really cared if I went to one of my friend's parties. Nor did it matter whether the friend was a boy or a girl. But, it was now a different culture. After some confrontation, arguing, and imploring, my mother and father gave me permission to go. When I went to school most of the girl's backed out of their promises to attend the party. Only five girls showed up. The party was great, and I went home early. The next morning my driver got hold of my mother while she was going to her office before I came down to go to school.

Driver:	*Madam, your daughter's intentions are not right.*
Mother:	*What do you mean?*
Driver:	*Madam, our young miss went to a party with hundreds of boys, where there were only four other girls. She was sitting very close to one boy.*
Mother:	*She is too young to do all that.*
Driver:	*Madam, I'm just informing you. After all, I have some responsibilities for this family.*
Mother:	*Okay! I'm getting late for my office. Anyway, keep me informed. If you see something else, tell me.*
Driver:	*Madam, I am a poor man, I can't follow her everywhere.*
Mother:	*Why not?*
Driver:	*First of all, I have to drive the car. So I don't have enough time to keep an eye on her. But I have a solution for this problem. You could hire my brother to drive the car from time to time. This would give me the time to keep an eye on the young miss. My brother is a good driver and as loyal as I am.*
Mother:	*Well, your brother is hired . . . end of all problems.*
Driver:	*Madam, like I said, I'm a poor man. And I have a big family. I can't follow your daughter on my own expense. It would be very expensive for me.*
Mother:	*Oh, you don't have to worry about the money. You can ask for it from me at any point in time.*

When I came down to go to school, I saw a very wicked smile on my driver's face. But I did not understand that he had done a cheap thing against me, and one that would burden my life for some time.

When I got to school everyone was playing and chatting with one another as usual. Everything was normal, too normal for my driver who later told my mother that I had been plotting to skip class and go somewhere with my friends. Later a friend invited her cousins and me to her place for dinner. My driver saw a chance to make some money. When I went home the driver said that I had used the opportunity to call up some unknown people using my friend's telephone. Mother believed him and did not even think of finding out what might actually have been the truth. Month after month the driver kept on giving my mother false information, and he filled her mind with poison toward me.

We were supposed to go on a school fieldtrip. My mother thought I was using the fieldtrip as a cover. She thought I was going some place with friends. I could not convince her that I was speaking the truth. She forbade me from going anywhere with my friends. She even restricted me from talking to boys. She felt that a boy and a girl could never be just friends. I didn't think that she was serious. She did not give me a reason for her decision. I did not know what the driver had been telling her.

One day, a short time later, I invited some friends over to my house. Some of them were boys. I thought, since they were coming to my house while my mother was there, that it would be fine, as we would be supervised. I was wrong. Mother got very annoyed and scolded us. Everyone was shocked and left right away. My mother was angry with me, and I was angry with her. I kept asking my mother for a reason for why she was restricting me in such a fashion. She would not give me a direct answer. She just kept on insisting that parents always do what is right for their children. Later, after even more problems, and lies from our driver, my mother became worried that I was using drugs, or was even a drug addict. With this misinformation, she limited my movements, keeping me from calling my friends, and only allowed me to go to and from school. I hated it. I protested. I pleaded my innocence, to no avail. My friends sympathized with me, at school they would simply tell me, "After all, this is Bangladesh." It took months for my mother to realize that what she had been hearing about me wasn't true. It took even longer for her to understand that I was interacting with my friends, and boys, as I had been used to doing in Canada. I wasn't doing anything improper. My mother was treating me harshly, I think, partially because of the Bangladeshi culture's pressure on her to insure that she was raising me properly according to the local standards.

What are those standards? Are they fair and right? The people I meet here, at least the adults, distinguish one another along gender lines. They don't look at the individual, or an individual's credibility. If you are a girl, in my opinion, then you inherit all the miseries of life. If you are a boy, then you are king of the world. This is how society deals with people in Bangladesh. Then come social caste and other divisions. In every division, there are splits in treatment between boys and girls. This hurts everyone.

In the future, if I have to compete for a job with a male, and even if that male is less qualified than me, I would lose the job to him. This is because it is considered unsafe for a woman to travel late at night and therefore women are not expected to work overtime here. If a woman works late, it is considered unbecoming and harmful to the social fabric. When a woman is over 18 and not yet married, parents worry about her prospects. When a man turns 18 his parents worry about his higher studies and how to make his life more comfortable. I think everyone should have a fair chance in life, be treated as equals, with equal expectations and responsibilities. If parents would have more faith in their children, both girls and boys, then Bangladesh would be a better place for everyone to live in. This country has advanced technologically, but it still has too many chains holding it to the past.

My parents are modern in that they want me to continue my studies and get advanced degrees, even though I am a woman. But, they have made mistakes raising me, and those mistakes, I think, were the result of pressure they felt from society. My parents and I have cleared up much confusion. We have grown to trust each other, but still, they fear for me, perhaps because they worry about how society will accept me. I have both suffered and enjoyed many changes in my life; everything has made me stronger and better. Bangladesh has suffered and enjoyed many changes, too. Things are getting better for women, and therefore, for society also. But, it is taking time and going at its own pace. After all, this is Bangladesh.

On a Hot Summer's Day

Sameeha Suraiya

The world outside lay absolutely motionless. Not a leaf on the trees stirred. Nature lay still and defenseless under the blanket of the August heat. Everything moving and alive seemed to have stopped, dazed under the blazing sun. I fought an unwilling battle to listen but my mind wandered.

I sat fidgeting in my chair, feeling restless. The teacher droned on and on. From the snatches of her lecture that I could make out, I understood it had something to do with fractions and decimals. Math. I wanted be anywhere but in that hot stuffy room. For reasons unknown the sun had decided to shine with all its might exactly on the spot where I was sitting. The wise fat bumblebee just outside my window buzzed on while the strong perfumed scent of the bougainvilleas mingled with the stifling air – I felt drowsy. The whirling fan above seemed to be taunting me by generating as much hot air as it could.

I looked outside the window to the narrow street that ran by. Birds perched on the electric poles, looking lifeless. A dog limped by, its red tongue lolling from sheer thirst. I looked for the street children who always devised countless noisy games. From the hot room that I struggled in, their lives seemed far better off than mine.

I thought of a gravity-free world where everything would fly right out through the window to oblivion. If only such a state existed, if only the mess of sheets in front of me, marked and remarked, the board with indecipherable symbols -- if only they would float up and disappear. I let my heat-addled mind flow wherever it wanted to take me. I thought of the anti-gravity force of my imaginary world and wished it would take me out through the window and fly me through the cool blue skies, as light as a feather, to all the cold places in the world. I would wrap my arms around the gusty, freezing wind. I envisioned myself on the vast ice fields of Alaska and before the mighty white glaciers. Yet, however hard I tried to transmit myself to those destinations, the heat stubbornly held me back.

The sharp ringing of the alarm snapped my mind back to the classroom. I looked at my watch and jumped with relieved delight – the dreadful class was over. But my newfound ecstasy was dashed to the ground when I saw what was written on the board. In big bold red letters the words glared out at me: "TEST TOMORROW ON TODAY'S TOPIC."

Encounter with the Prune
Mahreen Murad

It was Wednesday night and we were stuck in our room, forced to be with our books and each other – we preferred each other to books, naturally. Our mother made sure the television was switched off every school-day evening and not even my father could watch the news during those two hours. The house had to be silent. Any other day of the week we would be entertaining each other, inside the safety of our locked door, with comic acts of what our teachers did that day, but on a Wednesday we were always more subdued – our regular Thursday night journey to what we thought was the end of the world would be heavy on our puny minds. Children usually look forward to the last day of the week, but not us. We hated Thursdays more than we hated medicine without sugar.

We used to be like Jem and Scout Finch, my brother and I, and we almost literally had our very own Boo Radley. Only difference was it wasn't a man. She was our great grandmother, our paternal grandfather's mother. She had outlived my grandfather who had been killed at war, and she was the ancientest person we ever saw in real life.

Every Thursday night till the day she died we had to accompany our parents, dressed nicely, hair brushed neatly (mine in uncharacteristic pony tails) to visit HER. For some reason, I believe children fear very old people, especially very old wrinkly women. My brother and I were scared, I out of my ponytails, of her. We would dwell on our Thursday night routine from the night before, and I blame those visits for many restless nights.

As Thursday evening crept up, our smiles fled to the dark side of the moon and refused to show up even at the offer of chocolates. There would not be any of the usual chattering that could be heard whenever we went out somewhere and no one piped up, "Are we there yet," from the back of the car, where we sat stiffly and silently. Our mother would say, "You will go in and see your *Boro Ma* before you scamper off looking for the cats" and Father would add, "And don't even think of bringing one back with us, it's not happening so don't even try," but we would be too preoccupied about our encounter with the Prune to even think about the felines roaming all over the house.

We would always reach her house faster than we thought we had the last Thursday we were there, and we took as much time as we could to step out of the car without getting our ears pulled by our father. The front door was never locked at that house, and we were supposed to step right in. We wished there was a doorbell that had to be rung to buy us more time to settle the fear that was growing in the pits of our tiny tummies. Yet, that fear would always leave us momentarily as soon as father pushed the door open, and we would burst in, excited to see the cats and to be in that huge old house with its many nooks and crannies to investigate. We forgot for that one distracted second what lay ahead of us. But our excitement was always short lived once the realization that we had to rub noses with our grandmother hit us as our father herded us toward her room. My brother decided that the best way to do this chore was to run up to her and get it over with fast as possible. Me being the follower, I would just run next to him, trying to keep up.

As soon as we entered the her room the sharp wet smell of raw betel nut would reach our noses, which would crinkle immediately and sometimes just at the anticipation of it even when we were too far away to actually smell it, and we would see the large pointed hook of a nose looming at us, coming closer when we weren't moving. Fear would constrict our throats and the respectful *Salaams* would never come out right. I had to urge my feet to move closer and they often denied my requests until I would see a blob flash past me and back again out of the room. I would become inspired by my brother's speed and agility and try to do the same.

The operation was never as successful as my brother's. I would be there, my nose rubbing the big old prune, soft, wrinkly and moist and time would cease to move. The oily smell of snot and betel leaf sit would assault me and I would struggle to get away. On the verge of freedom, when I could even taste it in my mouth, an iron clasp would imprison me and I would think of death, as much as I knew of the concept.

There was no escaping that grip. No amount of wiggling could get me out and I would stand there, being sniffed all over my face. On my release I would rush to the bathroom to wash my face with soap and on my way I could feel the moist remnants of the *Shlheti kiss*, the affectionate "hunga."

I remember her nose, the smell and the fear even now, but I don't remember her death or being upset about it. I believe surviving those Thursday nights has made me a stronger person.

Why?
Idrak Hossain

Hope

Someone once told me that it is better to start a piece of writing with a quote, something good. So I am starting off this piece of little nonsense that is coming out of my cryptic mind with a quote from a greatly learned and respected man: William Shakespeare. According to him, "If music is the food for love...." (Shakespeare, *Twelfth Night*), then what is the food for life? Hope? Yes, I presume so. But if hope is the food for life then what really is life? I don't know and surely will never know because we, the humans, are 'rimmed' with something called a brain which is unsighted against all the 'known' and 'unknowns' of this world, combined or separate.

If

Life is something whose middle name is "if." It is something that will keep us regretting each and every single moment of it with a sense of "un-fulfillment" even during the moments of success.

Success

Although I have used the word success but what success really is, is something which I, or rather we, don't know. I have just put down the word by checking out its meaning from the book written by Dr. Johnson in the 17th century which is commonly known as the <u>dictionary</u>.

Risk

We are scared to pick up the chances and scared to "risk" life by taking chances when we know that we have nothing to lose, as we don't really have anything. We came into this world empty handed and we will leave this world empty handed. All we will leave behind are some snapshots in a photo album. Some will rejoice at our departure from this world and others will shed tears for a little while and then wipe off our short existence from the back of their minds.

Civilized

Have we ever wondered what is the meaning of the word *civilized*? Have we ever wondered why people beg, steal, rob, rape or murder? Have we ever thought of the child who saw his father die? Have we ever thought, "How will the 'hand to mouth' slum dweller survive if he is driven out of his 'residence'"? Have we ever wondered why we, the humans, are said to be the best creation of The Almighty? Many of us might directly shoot a stern answer "yes" but my earnest request to them is to be honest and true to themselves, to their heart and their inner soul, and think it over. HAVE WE? Please do think once again before again saying "yes." HAVE WE? We REALLY have? If so, then why are we unhappy or unsatisfied? Even now when we have the whole world in our grip with so many scientific inventions? Why do we try to improvise means to rectify our lives and why don't we stop in that act?

All the poets, writers, musicians and artists have wrung their hearts out to change our lives and restore peace upon the planet. A planet for which we were supposed to be blessed with but in reality we are cursed with. Why do we TRY? Why are we just a tool of our own invention? Why do we indulge ourselves in the bloody entertainment called war and just nod our head and saying "This is wrong?" Have we ever tried? REALLY TRIED? I don't know. I really don't know because I am just a "dilemma infected" creature who is just trying his best to find out the reason behind our existence, trying to find the meaning of the word **"life"** like a billion others.

THE SECOND WEEK:
POETRY

People write poetry for many reasons. Some write to record their pasts, to validate and to share their memories with family, friends, and classmates. Others write poetry to express feelings and support their own healing. For some, writing poems provides a deepening of their spirituality and their connection with others. Poetry writing expands a writer's creativity, and the principles of poetry enhance prose writing and speech. –Shelley Tucker, Writing Poetry.

Poetry is . . . *the rhythmical creation of beauty.* – Edgar Allen Poe
Poetry is . . . *a reaching out toward expressions, an effort to find fulfillment.* – Robert Frost
Poetry is the record of the best and happiest moments of the best minds, the very image of life expressed in its eternal truth. – Percy Bysshe Shelley

Poetry is a type of literature . . .
  ➢ In which words are selected for their beauty, sound, and power to express feelings.
  ➢ That uses a kind of language that is more intense and expressive than everyday speech.
  ➢ That presents the speaker's emotions as they are aroused by beauty, experience, or attachment.
  ➢ That provides a fresh, unexpected way of looking at things.
  ➢ That gives pleasure, whether it appeals to the senses, emotion, or intellect.
– Laurie Rozakis, The C.I. Guide to Creative Writing.

A poem should not mean
But be.
--From Ars Poetica by Archibald MacLeish

You must write approximately **forty** lines of poetry. This can be as one or two poems in free verse (or blank verse or any variety of rhyme schemes) and your *Poem of Myself.* If you choose to write a few haiku poems along with your *Poem of Myself,* you must try to match the number of lines required. Topics for your poems can range as far as your experience or interests allow.

A STATION AT NIGHT
Sameeha Suraiya

A cold night
Gloomy, desolate,
With a fire burning to warm
Body and soul.

A sense of despair shared 'round
They huddle together
Grimy and patched cloths wrapped
Around tired bodies
Dusk arrives and with it the morning train
As it creaks and groans to a halt –
Voices and footsteps everywhere
But nothing can stir the poor souls
Still in their deep slumber

CATASTROPHE
Sameeha Suraiya

Buildings crash
Like it was the end of the world
Skeletal remains – broken dreams
They stick out,
Piercing the gloomy sky.
Life never lived,
Lullabies shrivel and go unsung
Bony hands held out
Haggard sighs –
Echo in an unending symphony
Shrill alarms ring on –
They go unheeded
It is the end of the world.

I HAVE NO IDEA
Nasrin Akter

I have no idea
Why the world is so beautiful!
I have no idea
Why the sky is so blue!
I have no idea
Why the ocean is so clear!
I have no idea
Why the forest is so green!
I have no idea
Why life is rough!
I have no idea
Why I like you as I do and

I have no idea
Why I love you so much!

A POEM: MOI
Kashfi Ahmed

Moi
Kashfi means Inner Eye
--I can read what's on your mind
Just by the look in your eye
I can understand the heart inside

Daughter of Nasir
Dad, he loves to study
From childhood till today
I have been hearing him say
Study well; study hard
You have the potential to be a star

Lover of blue oceans
All that which lives under the surf
Wish to be a mermaid someday
To swim in my lover's chest
Of mystery blue, all the best
In the midst of warmth
Of grace, care -- love
I still feel different
a standout odd
Sometimes when things stay
The way they use to be
I feel in vain, useless and upset

'Cause I feel a need for change
Must come to people's mind
Loving, caring isn't enough
But a broad mind will crown us
With a wondrous land
That I dream to see
Somewhere, somehow
For I know one day this country will stand proud

I need music to sooth my soul
Instrumental, classical, and all
That leaves my soul in peace and rest
Quenches my thirst at its best

Freedom is a must
I shall cut thee apart
If denied liberty

It kills my joy
It is important
Not a toy

To give makes me fly
Fills my heart with absolute joy
Above the mountains, across the seas
Happiness fills me so much
Teaching the orphans
An experience apart

When little I was afraid
Of the corridors that lay
Silent and still, pitch black
There might be a Dracula turned into a bat
Waiting for me to walk alone
Would come to get me
To get my blood

A vision very different
Would like to see
The world shines
With peace and joy
At every piece of land
Stop bombing people
Let's cut those hands that do

Resident of Dhaka
A highly polluted space
But this is my origin
Mother Bangladesh
Ahmed, the prophet's name it has a meaning
That I cannot say
A holy name from God
I am proud, did you know?

A POEM OF MYSELF
Nur Bahar Alif

Light with brightness
Splendid meaning of my name
Has a spic and span feeling
Honesty and truthfulness give me gravity,
Childish speech proves simplicity
Softly, hear, a deep sense of gratitude.
Feelings of family, forever, eternal,
Uncle, aunt, grandpa, grandma,
Made the fountains of heaven
All around me.

I'm the lover of
Oceans, the sinuous grace of heart,
Greenery, ethereal beauty,
Sky, ostentatious cover of crimson roses.
Golden sun, redden breeze, feel me
A peacock blue night, ecstatic,
Moon of paradise, gorgeous.
I need . . .
Luminous eyes, illustrative,
Gentle voice, prestigious music,
Rhythmic fingers, a new star on the sky.
Pink dreams, great felicity of life,
Embrace me with great fervor,
Silver flavor, pleasing story.
I'm fearful of . . .
The creator of my soul,
Rudeness, jeers, and jealousy,
Crowd of people, heart beating!
Paucity of knowledge, same thing
She, the greatest lady "Ma"
Would like to see, I'm the
Best in her eyes.
He, beloved gentleman, "Baba",
Would like to see the heaven
Through my eyes.
A cute palace, living I'm
Decent lady with gorgeous ornaments,
Sweet music room-jhoom room-jhoom,
Beautiful and luxurious,
Dancing and singing with a smiling look.
Name is not fame but luck,
I'm lucky, everyone tells me,
The Fortune Girl.
The greatest feeling of my life.

POEM BASED ON
A SELF-CREATED METAPHOR
Alipha Khan

The moon is a spotlight.
It shines down on life
Highlighting, evaluating,
Analyzing each incident.
We are its subjects in focus.
The light is pointing at you.
Your moment of stardom,
A moment spanning a lifetime.

POEM CONNECTING THE WORDS-
JOY, COOK AND OUTER SPACE
Alipha Khan

Life is good today.
The diner across the street
Not exactly Spago's
But who's complaining?

As a kid, I wanted
To be an astronaut
- I grew up in the 60's
Watching "The Jetsons" on TV.

Outer space, little green men
They're my buddies today
So I'm not bounding through
The Milky Way
But who's complaining?

"Rodriguez's Culinary School"
Dad could never really be proud
Day after day creating pates
Far cry from the Apollo 13
Yet I'm not complaining!

THOUGHTS
Alipha Khan

Watch me do the tabletop moonwalk
Catching my breath in the lump in my throat.
See the materialists burn me down.
I saw them shaking the religion out
From the system, completely, forever.
But reality never brought on mirthful idealism.
The dreadful stains on the couch
The post-its on the fridge door
Everything in being suddenly makes sense
Albeit in a paradoxical way.........................

FOUND, LOST.....
Alipha Khan

In all but divine ecstasy
I was drifting blissfully
Lost in the clouds of fantasious wonder.....
When into the dream you came

And across the soft carpet of my reverie you walked
With hobnail boots.

Like a dead morning glory
In a garden of beautiful roses
I will live on as a disturbing memory
In the most profound of your fantasies.

UNTITLED
Alipha Khan

Suddenly tonight
I happened u'pon the moon
Or rather, the opposite.
Weary, not from overwork
Rather a day's worth of simple pleasures
Lost was I momentarily
In the deadly trap of reality.

A glance out the window
A luminous blur in the dark sky
I wouldn't be waxing poetic
The opal demigod wouldn't call out to me.

Mysterious mirage
Now so assailable
Unfazed, I looked on
At clouds wrapping lalune in their cobwebs.

DEATH BECOMES HER
Alipha Khan

Think not of me when the sun goes down
Dream not of me at night in your sleep…
Let not
That song
Remind you
Of me
Take no notice of the old photographs.
I HAVE LEFT YOU

Burn no candle for me on a Tuesday
Cry not for me during the rain…
Expect not
My return
To you
In this lifetime
Place no roses upon my grave.
I AM FREE NOW

TITLE-LESS
Alipha Khan

Come to me……turn, come to me
Watch me now…..awaiting you
Come to me……turn, come to me
Let me behold you with these eyes
Let me thread you a garland of tears
The tears that you'd bring into my eyes
When you'd come to me……..……..
And take me away, forever.

FREUD'S FIELD DAY
Alipha Khan

This desert has seen many sandstorms
this desert has seen much thunder
Let it build its fortress now
Never get this close to me.
Dangled, strangled, disentangled
Accept the joy I share with you
But, let my sorrow breed within my own walls.

SHADOW PUPPET
Alipha Khan

(Inspired by a cheesy text-message forwarded from a rather unusual source)

Dark, determined
unseen, until the inevitable
When I feel the sting
And watch my blood being fed upon……..

All the years that I'd lived the lie
the needles were just as painless
But they took more than my blood, my dear
but they took more than my blood.

Fooled by my predator
yet even more so by myself
Behind a silk screen,
I danced to the tune of my own demise……..

Tiny, fearless
Ignored, until the inevitable
when I see the swollen skin
And feel a part of me gone forever……….

The curtains get drawn
perhaps for the last time
I have finally joined the audience, my dear
I have finally joined the audience.

but the bump on my skin remains......
An eternal reminder
Of all that could have been avoided.
*(Mosquitoes, vampires in their own right & vampiric
people who drain you out by using you as a
toy to suite themselves . . .
which creature is more honest?)*

FALSELY MESMERIZE
Idrak Hossain

Floating on a shell
In a sea of questions
Purpose, Survival
Existence.
Shaping questions to heaven.
Need to tell
Untie the knot of confusions.
Seek an angel
Cannot reveal secrets.
Enigma broken on its head
Inside you he is dead.

THE END
Idrak Hossain

I walk down every street
And hear, hear hungry cries
I watch every, every street
And hear screech, screeching tires.

Weakened hearts cry out loud,
And wait for the bell to ring.
A Porsche owner plays the sound
And says Lamborghini was not his thing.

They arrest the *"parasytes"*
And the servants control the roots.
They stuff us with cheerful sights,
And we shower cries and woes.

Hopeless life in every being
The shrill voice sublimes everything.

WILD HORSES
Idrak Hossain

Raven 'n crows
Fly away
Reach heaven
Come
Array............
Teacups on tray
TV show begins
No game
Wild tame

OBSCURED
Idrak Hossain

Concealed deep inside
The feeling that's burning
It tries to break free
And reach the heavens
Like a wild Raven
And disclose the innocent sin
That has never really been
The true Devil's warning.
Let it always be obscured
And blue skies ensured.

PROMETHEUS UNBOUND
Idrak Hossain

We've got McDonalds, and
We've got hungry farmers.
We waste our flesh and meat
At the cost of heavy armors
And our servants dictate our sound.

We fall for exotic mystic richness,
Unaware of the reality
We succumb to oriental tempting beauty
With no idea of scarcity
And our slaves determine our ground.

DRIFTING AWAY
Idrak Hossain

There she lies
On the soft drifting sand,
Waiting to be embraced
By unselfish hands,
To tie the band.

Inseparable souls,
Like the hands
Of a compass;
The legendary comparison
By John Donne.

A RELIC OF MY PAST
Idrak Hossain

Crawling down the midst of this inevitable road,
I find myself climbing up the well
Of unpredictable instances of existence.
And with a dream to escape the visible hell.

Numbed by the striking sunlight of reality
That directs me to the bitter 'recognized'.
A ray pierced through the invisible hole
And I follow it to reach the end.

Memories leave me regretting the present
With the prediction of a dark future that waits
I seek pleasure in the swept away instances
And being just a relic of my past.

THREE HAIKUS
Kazi Sarmad Karim

From top to bottom
Falls the greenish, mosaic
Dark skinned

A sudden rush when
The birds are in ecstasy
While flying away

River of water
Falling from a tightly unscrewed
And expensive tap

MEMOIRS OF A REALIZATION
Kazi Sarmad Karim

A silence that pierces a thousand screams
A light that oozes darkness
Permeating the hopes of dreams
Resulting in a glaring nothingness

Washed away are the rays of hope
Clean as a whistle with nothing more
To freedom they always say "No"
Better this way for evermore

Streets full of empty souls
Fit and fine, they like it like that
Ready for molding in the coal
Any shape you want just like a doormat

A happy life full of sadness
Working like a buzzing bee
Collecting nectar without sweetness
Without even a mention of a fee

Be happy with a small family
And on the side a Mistress
Just like the TV family
That is ingrained in our brains

SEVEN EPIGRAMS
Kazi Sarmad Karim

Thoughts of a married man

The beauty of marriage
Exasperated in the ensuing barrage

A wise man once said "Marry and be well"
To that I always say, "I married and saw hell."

The love of my life, my car
I just never say I love it more than her

On love

They say, "Love is divine"
But never mention what gets left behind

Love is like the sweet cup of coffee in the morning
That burns everything inside!

Three simple words, "I love you"
Soon will they castrate you?

When you say, "I love you"
Never finish with
"More than my last beau"

HOW DO I HATE THEE?
Mahreen Murad
(*A Twist to the Poem, How do I love thee, let me count the ways . . .*)

How do I hate thee? Let me count the ways.

I hate thee at morning light
As thou crawls on my mosquito net
I hate thee with the passion of a heartbroken lover
As thou searchest with thy oily feelers

I hate thee from the bottom of my heart
And I hate thee even more
When thou skitters around my kitchen
And half way around the whole world.

THE
INEVITABLE TRUTH
Bushra Rahman

When I look at the sky, I see the sky
How blue the sky is!
The patches of clouds that are passing by
The golden sun that flashes light
Remind me all the time
I am alive, still breathing…

When I hear the coo-coo bird singing, I hear that song
How pleasant the song is!
The rhythm that floats on the air
Makes my heart dance with cheer
And it reminds all the time
I am alive, still breathing…

When I look at the moon, I see the moon
Hanging like a silver plate
Smiling back at me and
Showering the whole world
With silver rain.
She asks me to come and
Get wet silently…
I feel the bliss inside me
And my passionate heart reminds me
I am alive, still breathing…

The colorful butterfly with
Color on her wings
Flying and flying
Through the blooming flowers…
The green leaves, the buzzing bees,
The flowers' fragrance
Blending together
Make the spring more beautiful…
Touching my heart
Echoing inside me, and they

Remind me all the time
I am alive, still living…

My heart soars higher with passion
Feels everything moving as usual
As they will be afterwards
Maybe I will not live
A long time
And it makes me feel all the time
I am alive, still living…

I see them all, I feel the same
As I found even some days before
But you my dear
My dear friend
Remind me all the time
I will have to leave
Leave this world
As you have silently passed away…

WEEK THREE:
SHORT STORY

[A short story] . . . can be read in an hour and remembered for a lifetime.
-- Stephen Vincent Benet

A skillful literary artist has constructed a tale. If wise, he has . . . conceived, with deliberate care, a certain unique or single effect to wrought out, he then invents such incidents—he then combines such events as may best aid him in establishing this preconceived effect . . . In the whole composition there should be no word written, of which the tendency, direct or indirect, is not to the one pre-established design. – Edgar Allen Poe (1809 – 1849)

[The short story is] bits and pieces of life, the brightest and the darkest . . . Ideally, a short story is Life in a capsule. – Marian Gavin, author of The Sparrow's Mother.

You should complete the Short Story Outline along with one of these types of short stories:

- ❖ A children's story
- ❖ Something from your life that you "fictionalize"
- ❖ A vignette
- ❖ Create a character: use the characterization sheet and then put him or her in a situation/action scene where the audience will see and understand who this person is.
- ❖ Develop a tale about a life-changing experience.

Belonging

Kazi Sarmad Karim

As Akash came down from the taxi, the hot and humid air engulfed him from all sides. Tugging at his collar he opened the top button to let in some air. Getting some momentary respite he took out a 100 Taka note from his wallet to pay the fare. But the driver was not satisfied with the amount.

"Sir, if you do not pay us a little extra how will we live?" He asked earnestly.

"But the meter says 96 Taka; so I am already paying you extra!" replied Akash incredulously.

"Sir, it is nothing for you. But for me it means more food" said the driver slyly.

Akash, though unwillingly, paid the man the extra fare and brought out his luggage. His luggage consisted of one suitcase and a bag. He always liked to travel as light as he possibly could. But this trip was different so he had a suitcase as well as his usual bag. He slung the bag over his shoulder and headed to the entrance of the rail station. He let out a sigh thinking of just how the driver had swindled him a moment ago. It had been so long since he had bargained like that, that he had lost his power to bargain. Then he chuckled in spite of himself, at least now I definitely feel like I am in Bangladesh.

He looked at the entrance to the Komolapur Rail Station and felt the memories flooding back. It felt like just yesterday he had arrived at the station for the first time and been overawed by it. Coming to Dhaka from Comilla by train was the hardest thing he had ever done. But there was also tremendous pleasure and wonderment at the thought of living in the big city as an adult. The wonder he had experienced then was measurable only to the wonder he had experienced when he got the visa to go to the US.

Twenty years later, he felt a sense of déjà vu staring at the entrance to the station. But he also felt that something was not right. He went inside the station and went to the ticket counter. He bought a ticket for Comilla and sat on a nearby chair. He looked at the chair and saw it was bright red in color and very new looking. He smiled, thinking of the chairs that they had when he was a frequent traveler between Dhaka and Comilla. But then he thought a lot would have changed in twenty years. I certainly have changed, he mused looking at his reflection in the glass. A casually dressed man, in an expensive Calvin-Klein shirt and sporting new Nike sneakers looked back at him. "Times change, people change," he thought, understanding the deep meaning of the adage.

A train had just arrived and he saw a flood of people swaying though the crowd to the exit. He watched them filter through and thought to himself, that one day he himself had gone through here to face the world. He smiled again thinking to himself, that even in his wildest dreams he had never contemplated that he would graduate with a Masters in Electrical Engineering from MIT. He took a sip from his MUM bottle and opened a bag of Doritos that he had in his bag. Doritos was his favorite junk food and some of his friends joked that he was addicted to it. As Greg would say, "Akash the Doritos Man, la-de-da," he thought, humming silently.

But as he sat there eating and watching the flock of people going to and fro inside the station, he suddenly had an epiphany. He realized that everyone inside the station seemed to have a purpose to his or her walk. Everybody was doing their own things, being totally immersed in their individual lives. He alone was the only one sitting and observing everything. He felt like he did not belong in this place where everybody knew his or her purpose and function. He stood out like a sore thumb.

He took out his American passport and looked at it. He looked up to see a few people staring at his passport with a look of awe and surprise. He silently thought to himself that they did not know how lucky they actually were. He realized that he was a stranger in his own country and that he belonged to no place. Just one thought kept ringing in his head, "I'm homeless!"

An Honest Shepard: A Story for Children
Nur Bahar Alif

Once upon a time there lived a king and queen in the city of Zuba. The city was rich with mesmerizing gardens of bougainvillea, where dewdrops shimmered in colorful, luxurious beauty. Rosy soft breezes danced in the leaves and smiling, sparkling stars gave light in the evenings to the majestic view. But such beauties could not attract attention of the king and the queen, because they had no child, and this grieved them greatly. They were impatient for a baby; so they prayed, "Oh, Lord, please give us a child."

One night the king was walking through the garden with the queen, enjoying the beauty of the fireflies twirling in the moonlight. Suddenly he saw a cute little fairy in front of him. She wore a silver dress that seemed to be sewn with diamonds, a gold tiara, and had golden hair whose ringlets fell below the purple sash at her waist. She held a chaplet of pansy flowers, which she presented to the king, and said, "Dear king, let the queen wear this chaplet as a crown and within a fortnight she shall conceive a child."

The fairy's words were true and the queen did conceived. Everyone was very happy to hear the news. They sang, "The cradle of snow drops waiting for the sparkling moon moments of pearls will smile soon."

At last the sweet little princess came into the world, her blue eyes were like the sea shimmering in the sunlight. Seeing her angelic beauty, everybody thought the moon had come to visit their land, and they sang, "You the princess of roses, you the most beloved have come to the door of our hearts!"

The king gave her the name Zubayda. When Zubayda became one year old the king arranged a party and invited the entire kingdom. Zubayda got many, many, gifts. It seemed that everyone was happy. Yet, there was one who was angry, one who the king had mistakenly forgotten to invite to the birthday party.

On the next evening, while the king and queen were playing with Zubayda, the fairy who gave the fateful flower crown to the king came to him and said, "Dear king, I am feeling disgraced -- you did not invite me to the party. This after all I did for you! For this insult I will see that Zubayda will soon die!"

Hearing this, the king deeply repented of what he had done, and said, "Dear fairy do not be angry, I am very sorry, please forgive me and spare my daughter."

The fairy said, "In as much as you are repentant, I pardon you, but on one condition."

"What condition dear fairy?" asked the king.

She explained that on the day that the princess turned sixteen years old she would fall asleep for many years. She said, "One day an brave and honest man will come and awaken her. He will be of humble background. You must see that he becomes the princess's husband, when this is done my curse will be finished. However, the man who awakens her must first complete a dangerous task."

The king thanked the fairy and gave her a tearful farewell.

The fairy did not lie. On her sixteenth birthday Zubayda was sewing a handkerchief for her dream prince. She pricked her finger on a needle, and fainted away, asleep. The king realized that all was happening as the fairy foretold, and so he summoned his ministers to announce to the kingdom that whoever could wake the princess from her slumber would be greatly rewarded but, when informed of the danger, nobody wanted to take the risk. All knew the danger that existed in a fairy given task. All cowered at the prospect. The king was upset. What will be done now? He again prayed, "Oh lord forgive our ignorance and return our child please . . . Summon a brave and honest man to come to me and rescue my child."

In the meantime, Sulaiman, who was a shepherd, and was eulogized as being exceptionally truthful and honest, heard the news. He spent his time with his flock, but was lonely. To ease his loneliness, he created melodies on his flute, pretending that he was playing for a beloved lady, the lady of his dreams. His music fascinated the birds, hills, and even the ocean. At night he dreamt emerald dreams and diamond thoughts and beautiful songs filled his heart, mind, and soul. He dreamt of the night sky and rubies. He dreamt of clothing his beloved in the raiment of the night. He dreamed of ermine and silk and precious furs and garments, all to be gifts for his beloved lady. These dreams gave him much pleasure and he transformed them all into song. Dreams and music sustained him, but still he desired a companion to share his life.

One rare day, when Sulaiman went into the town to take some of his sheep to the market, he heard the announcement of the king. That was his answer! He could awaken the princess and his life would no longer be lonely. He started to think, "How could I break the princess's spell?" He decided to visit the king. When he reached the king's palace, he met the king. The king was in a dark mood due to his daughters condition. Sulaiman told the king his intentions. The king advised him to go back home, as the task was very dangerous and he was but a simple shepherd boy, but Sulaiman responded confidently, "Dear King, do not worry just pray for me, and let me go."

The king was delighted with the bravery of Sulaiman. He prayed for him, and told him that soon a fairy would appear soon and assign him a dangerous task. This done, he sent him on his way.

The whole night, Sulaiman could not sleep. He just thought about his mission. Suddenly the fairy that gave the crown to the king came to him and told him, "You must catch a golden deer. It lives in a dark jungle next to a black mountain. But it is swifter than any man, more swift than any horse, no one has every caught it, indeed, if you draw near it, though that would be nearly impossible, it will strike at you with its antlers, each of which exudes a poison. A poison of instant death," Sulaiman gulped, then he remembered his manners and thanked the fairy for the warning.

The next morning Sulaiman started his journey. He took only his flute with him. When he reached the jungle by the black mountain, he saw a beautiful golden deer dancing, prancing, and running about. He tried to catch it but failed. It was as swift as the fairy had said. At last he decided to play music on his flute. The music enchanted the deer. It ceased running, turned, pricked up its ears, and then slowly, cautiously, it walked back to where Sulaiman sat beneath a tree. The deer knelt and placed its head in Sulaiman's lap. Sulaiman had caught it successfully. All at once the deer transformed itself into the very fairy that had told him of his task. Sulaiman was amazed to see this.

The fairy acknowledged his skill, courage, and wisdom. She gave him a ring of silver and told him to place it on the princess's finger. Sulaiman took the ring, thanked the fairy, and went back to the king's palace. He went to the princess's room, and approached the bed where the princess slept. He knelt down, gently picked up her hand, and slid the ring onto her finger. She stirred. Opening her eyes, she gazed at Sulaiman and fell in love. She took the handkerchief she had been sewing before her fateful pinprick, kissed it, and presented it to Sulaiman. Sulaiman thanked her and then went back to the king.

The king was overjoyed and wanted to reward Sulaiman. But still, father that he was, he wanted to test the young man's intentions. He wanted a son-in-law who would marry his daughter out of love, and not out of an interest in inheritance. He told Sulaiman, "Dear Sulaiman, I am grateful to you. I would like to reward you, what do you want."

Sulaiman answered, " Dear King, your justice is my reward."

"Thank you, Sulaiman, I want to make you my son-in-law," the king said, "Would you be happy if that were so?"

Sulaiman was surprised, but humbly inquired of the king, "Dear king I am happy but I am not rich. I have nothing accept a little house, twenty sheep and a flute. Will Zubayda be happy with this?" Sulaiman's truthfulness touched the king.

"I know my daughter, and she would be happy even under those conditions for she loves you. However, you will not live humbly. You will live in the palace and, when I am gone, you will be king," the king explained. Then he blessed the union.

Zubayda and Sulaiman became husband and wife, and they lived, of course, happily ever after.

Truthfulness and honesty are always rewarded.

Mina & Rina:
An Allegorical Tale
Shaima Laskar

Once upon a time there was a couple, Karim and Dina, both of whom where doctors. They were successful, but they were not happy because they did not have any children. One day Dina went to the church and asked God, "Why don't you give me any children?" She was crying and an angel who was passing by asked her, "Hey, why are you crying so much?" Dina answered that she was very unhappy and her life was empty without children so she wanted children at any cost. "At any cost?" asked the angel. "Yes," responded Dina, "at any cost!"

The angel thought for a while and told her that she will have children. However, one child will be so good that she will be happy and proud to be a mother and the other child would be so bad that she would regret having children, period. Dina was not quite sure where this angel had come from, but she accepted the bargain without another thought. She was very happy and she felt that she would never regret having a bad child. The main thing was she wanted children. After a few days Dina was pregnant. Her husband and all their friends and relatives were happy to hear the good news. They were especially excited when they heard that she would have twins. After a few months, Dina became very weak and ill so for special care Karim took her to a popular clinic and she stayed there waiting anxiously for their newborns to come into the world.

Dina and Karim were delighted to see their twin daughters. When they took them home Dina gave them names similar to her own: Mina and Rina. All of their friends and relatives were happy to see such beautiful twins.

Nobody except Dina could "identify" them properly when it came to their physical appearance. But, as Mina and Rina grew it became obvious that they were completely different in personalities. Mina was naughty, destructive, and greedy. On the other hand, Rina was calm, creative, and kind. Mina always made trouble at school but Rina was very good at school. She was always first in her exams and not only that she helped her mother at home with her household tasks. Mina was bad in her studies and she never helped her mother at home. She was always known as a bad girl.

When they were teenagers the trouble deepened. Whenever Mina did bad things outside she told them that she was not Mina but was Rina. They looked so alike that no one could prove she was not who she claimed to be, and, for that reason, whenever Rina went outside people thought that she was Mina and they treated her like a thief. For example, one day Mina tried to steal an expensive shirt. The manager of the shop caught her before she was able to get away. He took the shirt from her and demanded to know whom she was. She said, "I am Rina, the daughter of Dina and Karim, and you have a shoddy store and an ugly face!" The manager angrily kicked her out and ordered her to stay away from his store or next time he would call the police. Later, when Rina innocently went to the same store the manager yelled that she was a thief and chased her from his shop. After that Rina came home and told her mother what had happened.

Mina really enjoyed doing these things and hurting her sister's reputation because Mina did not like Rina for her goody-goody image. Dina was very upset and tired about Mina and she ordered Mina to go away from her house. Mina left, but the problems she caused did not end there. After some years Rina became a doctor like her parents, and Mina joined a gang and became a gang leader.

One day Mina and her gang killed a police officer and the police came to Dina's house to arrest Rina because Mina told the police that she was not Mina she was Rina. So the police took Rina to the police station. Dina could not rescue her innocent child, Rina, from her bad child, Mina.

Dina again went to the church and asked God, "Why did you give me such a bad child like Mina?" While she was crying the angel from long ago appeared again and answered. "Dina! My child, if God does not give you anything willingly than why do you force him to give it to you. If you force him than he will have to give it to you even though it is not pleasant for you." From that day Dina realized that she should not have forced God to give her children.

Caged for Life
Sameeha Suraiya

Man is the most hateful species that ever set foot on this earth. Man and I – an infinite and inseparable breach sprawls between us. He is the only real enemy I have.

I remember waking up to the shrill twittering of my mother, the note of fear and alarm evident. There was commotion in the darkness. I could feel the tension in the air. It was almost palpable. I perched, terrified, as I felt something sticky trickling down on my feathers. Horrified, I discovered I could no longer move. The raised voices of men rang out on all sides, but I could no longer hear my mother by my side. "Is this how the world is supposed to end?" I thought. I could only wait, my heart pounding. Just as I thought it was to beat its last, the voices stopped talking and then – a snap! I found myself falling out of my warm nest and into the cold hands of a big, burly man. I lay paralyzed in his strong grip. The sticky thing on my wings made it impossible for me to struggle. I kept up my high-pitched cries – that was all I could do. That was the last time I saw my home. It was also a farewell to my freedom.

Even before I had learned to fly with those wings, I was shut up in a cage. I do not know what those people found so special about me; they kept pointing to my blue-green wings. The first few days, I acted defiant. I felt exposed with so many pairs of eyes riveted towards me. I yearned to take a flight up into the blue skies and look down on everything. The sense of power I used to have over man as my mother guided me – yes, it was that power that I longed to win back.

I kept playing the memory of the last night of my freedom. I asked myself a lot of questions and the only conclusion that I reach is that man is a baffling species. They are a selfish species, too. They are even known to kill one of their own race in cold-blood! What are they thinking? They are obsessed in their need to control each other.

I just cannot fathom what pleasure they get in imprisoning a bird in a cage. They hang us in balconies and give us names that do not mean anything. When neighbors come, with great pride they announce the price tag attached to us, as though their self-identity depends upon it.

Man and beast should be living in peaceful co-existence. It is man who destroys the balance through the wars he wages against beasts and against each other. In the end, we are all wounded for eternity, as we dissolve away into nothingness.

Excerpt from a Prankster's Portfolio
Alipha Khan

The plan was simple enough. The concert was on Tuesday, which meant that there would be no one there on Monday-which was a public holiday. The cleaners would have cleaned and arranged everything by Sunday afternoon. All we had to do was break into the compound and then into the auditorium on Monday night, set up the canisters and cartons, and figures out all the light switch cables. The rest could conveniently be done during the show.

Sakib was the first to disagree when Omar hatched the plan, but we soon got him back on track. He's one of those louts who do every possible misdeed under the Solaris but then hide it so well that not even the most experienced authoritarian would ever consider suspecting him. Come to think of it, I suppose we're all like that…. anyways, back to the point. The raison d'être for Sakib's sudden urge to join the Pussycat Clan was this: he was one of the volunteers at the concert. Which meant he would have to be the principal miscreant. Which meant he would have to do most of the work. Which in turn meant, needless to say, if anything went wrong, he would be expelled from school – leading to the inevitable icing on the venom-laden cake; his retired Army officer dad ecstatically practicing every sadistic act he picked up during his days in the force on the much-deserving descendant. Well, now that he was in, our only concern was any bit of the game plan going even the slightest bit wrong.

****

Monday evening was here before we knew it. The sheer excitement at the prospect of what we were about to achieve made me turn down a third helping at dinner; an event measuring, in terms of commonness, the same likes as a public servant willing to forego the provisions of a promising act of bribery: my younger brother got hiccups out of shock. After midnight I snuck out with our Premio, an accomplishment I've mastered skillfully. After picking up Adnan and Omar we headed to Fazle's, where he and Sakib waited with the supplies. They were loaded into the trunk – we all prayed for the love of God for the eggs not to crack – and we were off.

For all its hype, dodging the security at the venue was a breeze. We left Adnan outside on guard, chiefly because he was too much of a lardarse to make it over the wall. Omar's skeleton key got us into the vast auditorium and we got started right away. Fazle worked the electric cables while the rest of us strategically positioned the eggs on the confetti-releaser and the fog canisters behind the loudspeakers. After going through the whole plan one last time, we were out again. The only thing we were scared of now were the RAB patrol cars: there was no reason why they wouldn't find anything fishy about a bunch of 17-year-old guys smoking pot and driving through the highway at top speed at 3 a.m. Luckily, we made it home without any mishap.

****

So came the fateful Tuesday afternoon. We got there before most people, and did everything as if we had no idea about what was going to happen. The bands would play in this order: Breach, Vibe, Fulbanu's Revenge, Watson Brothers, Kraal, Bivishika, Birodh...and then our target, Rezwan's band's very first stage performance. This made it really convenient, as we could all come out with clean consciences since we wouldn't be mucking up any of the others' performances.

The other bands played. It was mostly a typical so-dubbed Dhaka "underground" concert: minor mishaps with sound systems and very-high-hence-very-out-of-sync guitarists, thudding bass a tad too vibrant for comfort, the head banging "yo" wannabe crowd up front, the girls so dolled up it seemed they were at a formal dinner, the distinct smell of invisible weed, the ever-annoying clicks of cell phone cams – the Full Monty. When Birodh got on stage, I saw Sakib moving towards the stairs leading right above the stage. The dude was smart – he carried a bunch of fliers as if he was busy with volunteer errands. Soon he disappeared behind the cardboard backdrop.

Birodh left the stage, and Arafat Bhai from Watson Brothers introduced Rez's band. The puswits started with "Iris", and then did Creed's "Higher." We waited. After sometime, we got to work. Fazle was already outside.

"Thanks people. Now we'd like to share one of our own compositions with you. This one's called *Porinoti*."

I couldn't help but smirk at the irony. The second the song started, the lights were out and the smoke from the canisters filled the room. Sakib let go of the confetti string, landing the 25 dozen eggs we bought half-price from Omar's uncle's poultry farm all over the bewildered band and their showy, pricey equipment. Then something completely unexpected happened – the excessive smoke set off smoke detectors we hadn't seen before, resulting in a shower that added further depth to the panic and confusion. Everyone was rushing to the narrow exit door. The other bands and the organizers tried to calm the mob, to no avail. Rez and his crew were stupefied, trying to figure out where the eggs came from.

****

Clichéd as it may sound, nothing tastes as sweet as victory. We figured leaving with the crowd would divert suspicion away from us. The moment we were out, we shuffled to the parking lot, made a mad dash for the car and scrammed.

Keeping a car on the road is very hard if you are laughing till your insides ache. It is also very hard to pay attention to other traffic. That is basically what happened when I rammed the car onto the back of a Pajero. The result? Smashed headlights, a crunched-up car boot, a collapsing Pajero bumper (i.e. several months' pocket money) and five lumps on five heads with a few sprained elbows thrown in.

Heck, it was all worth it.

10 Minutes in a Bar
Idrak Hossain

"Hey! There she is!"

"Now go and ask her cell or land number, Sami! Just staring at each other 'n passing some mysterious out-of-the-known-freaking-world smiles won't help."

The strange mysterious music and the weird, hazy and smoky surroundings engulfed them. The darkness outside seemed to pull them towards some mysterious destination and the girl seemed to be the sorceress of it. But none of them could move, especially Sami. He was glued to his seat and the luscious yet innocent eyes of the girl and the heavenly smile seemed to steal his soul.

"May I help you?" the untimely intervention of the bartender pulled the puppet string and brought them back to the bar from their strange world of unwanted fantasies! Sami and Aysha both gave a stir and looked at each other.

"Yeah! eeeerm….I'll have two shots of Absolute. What 'bout you, Ash?"

"Orange juice with just a little kick."

"Pheewwwwww!' exhaled Sami. "Wow, I don't know what's wrong with me but I somehow get lost whenever I look at that gal."

"You loser, you can only look 'n smile and get lost! That ain't gonna help. This is the third day, damn. Now go n………..," saying this Aysha turned to see the girl and shouted.

"Sams… Look!"

"What happened?" Sami turned around and exclaimed, "She's gone! Damn! This is the third day I almost got hold of her 'n let it slip through my fingers!"

"Bad luck! Sheer bad luck! You've missed her again!"

"Yeah Ash," the sadness in his voice got distinct this time.

"It's strange how you fall in love with someone by just seeing him or her! Sams, dear, you're P-A-T-H-E-T-I-C."

"Thanks Ash," Sami seemed to blush a bit.

"Let's hit the road Ash! These people take ages to serve the drinks."

"You sure! I wanna go for a few rounds before I leave. Let's wait for a while, Sams."

"We'll have a few rounds at the hotel, Ash."

This is their third day in London. They live in Dhaka. They are best friends since childhood. They are actually family friends. Or rather they were family friends when they had had a family. When Aysha's parents died Sami's parents raised her. After Sami's father's mysterious death and his mother's unexpected suicide, they have been living together. Fortunately, Sami's father left him a handsome fortune.

The night was pitch dark. It was also drizzling. In this town, where the streets have no lights and when the crescent moon is hidden behind heavy black clouds, it is difficult to see the person who's next to you. No, it is not the ideal night for vampires to haunt. Even the bravest vampire would not think to venture out on a night like this. And moreover how will they haunt with the absence of moonlight and streetlights? What force is pulling Sami and Aysha to take a walk on a night like this? It is a mystery such that would be a daunting task for even Sherlock Holmes to solve!

In the dark the roads never seem to end. While walking, suddenly a strange awareness struck Sami and he stared at Aysha who was walking just next to him. A loud thunderclap suddenly struck and at that instance, and in the light of a great lightening flash he saw a skeleton, drenched in blood and wearing Aysha's clothes waking beside him. Blood was dripping from the bones like rain. It looked like a walking human who has just been skinned and defleshed. Within a few seconds the skeleton suddenly burst into flames.

"N-a-a-a-a-a……….."

Aysha turned towards Sami.

"What happened Sami? What's wrong?"

"Oh! Ash………….I thought…I thought…I…. just saw a …"

"Saw what Sams?"

"Well… nothing. Forget it…I don't feel like walking. Let's grab a cab and get back to the hotel room."

Sami felt like revealing the dreadful figure he saw. He wanted to tell Aysha that he saw her burning -- burning in flames like a biblical character. But something stopped him from doing it.

From a distance the bargirl saw the whole incident. She has kept an eye on both of them for a while. When they both turned back to return to their hotel room, a grin was visible on her face. In the darkness, her eyes, which were shinning like the stars, were very visible.

Back in the hotel room, where the two friends resided, things somehow were not going right. Nothing was going their way. When they went to bed, no matter how much Sami tried, he couldn't sleep. The blood-dripping figure kept flashing back to his mind. Although he was awake, he hoped that it was just a nightmare. "Everything will be over once he opens his eyes and a brand new day will be waiting to welcome him and offer a grand start," he thought. The more he tried to concentrate on something else, the more strongly the unwanted memory kept flashing back.

Everything was dead silent. Nothing could be heard except the swirling of the fans and breathing. After a while, Sami decided to have a drink. "At least that would settle my nerves," thought Sami. He was dying for a sound sleep. He wanted to wipe off the figure he had imagined, and thought shockingly real, from the back of his mind forever. He got up from his bed, went to the fridge and grabbed a can of Heineken. Sami opened the can and took a sip. He lifted the can to his lips to take another sip. As he was taking the second sip he heard a shrill cry. Before Sami realized anything Aysha flung the door open and ran out of the room and headed towards the entrance and exit gate of the hotel. Sami, with no idea of what was going on started to chase her.

"Ash, Ash stop! What's the matter? STOP!"

But Aysha would not stop. Her eyes were lifeless. She seemed like a human stone, a stone that was freshly carved out to give birth to a moving statue. After running down to the end of the passage and near the gate, the guard, hearing the shouting tried to stop Aysha and bumped against her. The guard, a wall of a man, was thrown from the spot. Aysha stood there, unmoved, like a statue. The paleness in her face suddenly disappeared with an uncharacteristic slowness.

"Ash?"

Aysha gave a stir and turned slowly, very slowly towards Sami.

"Yes, Sami?" she asked.

"What's wrong, Ash?"

"I don't know what the hell I am doing here, Sams. I don't know. I just got the feeling that I wasn't me for a while. And I had no control over myself. After that I don't remember anything. How…why…what am I doing hear instead of the room?"

"Don't worry about that. Let's go and sleep."

Sami slowly guided Aysha to the room. They both went back to their beds and kept on repeating their vain attempt to sleep. Outside someone was looking at them through the window. It was the girl they saw at the bar. Her pale, white, bright and shining-like-the-jeweled-moon face would have surely caught the attention of Sami or Aysha if they had let an accidental glance slip towards the window. But they were staring at the ceiling. Puzzling fear and tiredness were fighting inside them. At last it was their tiredness that won and their eyelids were pulled down. As their eyelids were about to get drawn, they heard a sinister laugh outside – the sound of satisfaction of someone accomplishing some devilish work. The darkness seemed to get even darker with the laughter.

"HA-HA-HA-HA-HA………."

Their bones froze at the sound of the laughter and they yanked their eyelids up.

"Oh God! Help me! Help me! Get me out of this hallucination! Please pull the curtains of this nightmare," Sami and Aysha pleaded in their minds. They were not having a nightmare. But was it a hallucination? They both were rational persons. They both were science graduates. They did not believe in ghosts. They did not believe in the paranormal. So it must have been a hallucination. With this thought their exhaustion claimed a victory and they slept at last.

The morning wore a pleasant look. The first ray of the sun was strong, but not enough to break through the curtains of their windows. Suddenly there was a soft knock at their door. The knock was probably too weak to wake them up from their sleep and the "knocker" had to knock at the door again, this time a bit louder so that they would wake up from their sleep. Aysha slowly raised her head from her pillow and asked, "Who is it?"

"Your breakfast!"

"Oh come in."

The hotel boy came inside the room with a trolley loaded with food. Although they had had a hectic night they had no appetite. Aysha had a strange feeling of not being herself and Sami was thinking about the dreadful bloody figure he saw the other night and Aysha's strange behavior. There was dead silence in the room when Aysha broke it by saying, "You know something Sami? Last night I had no idea what was happening. I tried my best to sleep but the moment I was closing my eyes I saw a figure drenched in blood telling me that it was time to strike."

"I heard strange laughter," was Sami's short reply.

After saying those words, Sami realized that his stomach was grumbling for food, and he started eating his breakfast. Sami pushed a spoonful of cornflakes in his mouth. The cornflakes did not taste good, though. It tasted slimy, juicy and bitter. For just a second Sami looked at the bowl of cornflakes and saw worms were crawling out of the bowl of milk. A tiny worm also glided out of his mouth.

"Y-A-A-A-K-K-K-H-H-H!" He spat out the cornflakes.

"What happened?" asked Aysha.

"They served us worms!"

"Where?" Aysha looked at the bowl and saw fresh cornflakes. Sami also looked into the bowl and saw cornflakes swimming in milk.

"NO! Yeah right. But I tasted and saw worms!"

Sami looked at the bowl of cornflakes. No! There were no worms there. Then what did he see?

"I'm gonna take a shower," said Aysha and went to the bathroom. She turned on the shower tap, rinsed her body under the shower, rubbed body gel all over and stood under the shower for a long time to let all the foam washed off. Then she took the shampoo and started to rub it into her hair. While she was rubbing the shampoo on her head she felt an irregular lump. "A pimple on my skull? Weird," thought Aysha. Aysha didn't pay much attention to the pimple and started working on washing her hair with the shampoo. But the pimple irritated her more and more and she felt that it was growing bigger. Out of curiosity, Aysha stepped out of the shower and looked in the mirror trying to see the lump. It was difficult for her to see anything through her thick locks of hair. Failing to see the lump she again stood under the shower. The water seemed to wash off her weariness. It was refreshing indeed. While she was wiping off the water from her body she again felt the lump on her skull. She looked at the mirror to see what it was. As she was moving her hair to one side to have a clear look at the lump, in the reflection of hers in the glassy material, she saw a finger. She closed her eyes and looked at the mirror again. The finger was no longer there. "What's happening to me?" thought Aysha. As she was turning around to get out of the bathroom, something caught her attention. She again looked at the mirror and she saw a bloody hand coming out of her skull!

"A-A-A-A-H-H-H-H!"

"Ash, are you okay?" Sami's voice seemed far away. Aysha slowly opened her eyes.

"Everything is normal," said the doctor.

"What happened?" Aysha asked groggily.

"You fainted in the bathroom, Ash."

"I'll leave now. Just don't move about. Take a rest, I will be back in a little while with some medicine," saying this the doctor left the room.

"Come doctor, I'll walk you out," Sami went to the front door, opened it and waited for the doctor to leave the room.

"Sami come here."

"Tell Ash."

"What is happening with us, Sams?"

"I don't know Ash."

"Have we done something wrong for which we are being attacked continuously by some evil spirit?"

"C'mon Ash we have………."

Z-A-A-P

Suddenly Aysha struck Sami right in the middle of his head with an axe. She didn't know from where the axe came from but she felt it in her hand and felt like hitting Sami with it. And she did. Blood spurted out. Brains spilled all over the floor and bed. Some covered Aysha's face. Aysha's eyes suddenly turned bright. She pulled out the axe, pushed her hands through the bloody gate she created in Sami's skull and with all her force peeled off his skin. Then she dipped her finger into Sami's brains and put the finger in her mouth to taste it.

"Fresh metropolitan blood! M-U-H-A-H-A-H-A-H-A-H-A!"

There was a knock at the door. Aysha looked up. There was no axe and no dead and bloody Sami. To her relief she found out that it was not Sami whom she had chopped with the axe rather she had cut her palm with a pair of scissors. Where the scissors came from she wasn't sure. Blood covered the floor.

Aysha slowly stood up and walked towards the door. She was leaving trails of blood as she stepped towards the door. Aysha opened the door and to her terror saw the girl from the bar in front of her. The girl's jaw was hanging by a thin skin of her cheeks on one side. Her other cheek was completely missing. Her cheekbones and parts of her skull were exposed. A fountain of blood was dripping out of her. It seemed that if someone just nudged her, her jaw would fall off.

"N-O-O-O-O-O-O-O-O-O………………"

"What's the matter Ash?" the bloody girl hissed from the back of her throat.

"How the hell do you know me?" thought Aysha, but instead of speaking, she acted and stabbed the scissors right through the girl's shoulder.

"H-E-L-P!"

After putting the scissors through the girl's shoulder the madness that clutched Aysha was over and she came to her senses. She saw Sami on his knees with the scissors forced through his right shoulder. Responding to Sami's cry for help, and the screams of a few witnesses in the hallway, all the guards of the hotel came running and gathered around Sami who had fainted and lay sprawled in a growing pool of blood. Aysha was pulled out of the room. She was seeing and hearing everything but was comprehending nothing. She was spellbound.

"No officers, believe me, she didn't do it on purpose. She's very ill. She has to go back to the room and take a rest. She's under medication," Sami was making his case to a couple of cops. Aysha heard this conversation as if it was being held miles away.

Suddenly the "unsleeping" Aysha came to her senses.

"Sams what are we doing hear in this police station. WHAT are we doing here?"

"But everybody saw her stabbing you," stated the inspector.

"But sir you have to understand, she is ill, even a bit psychologically. She is under medication," explained Sami.

"Can you prove this?" asked the inspector.

"Here have a look at the prescription," saying this, Sami took out the prescription and handed it to the inspector. The police inspector had a thorough look at the prescription. Failing to make anything out of it because his profession was not to read prescriptions, he called up a doctor and checked everything with him. Then he turned to Sami and said, "How do I know that she isn't a threat to any other civilians?"

"She isn't," assured Sami. "Can we leave now?"

"Yes, but we will be checking up on the two of you to make sure that all remains well, if there are any more problems with her mental state, we may have to take her into custody to protect you and, of course, her," explained the inspector.

"What the hell is going on?" shouted Aysha. "And why do you have a bandage on you shoulder Sams? And why do I have a bandage on my palm, too, Sams?"cried out Aysha.

"Nothing Ash. Let's go to the hotel now."

On their way back, Aysha was continuously asking Sami about everything but Sami ignored her. When they reached the hotel, Sami and Aysha's saw the pool of blood on the floor. Sami quickly called the guard and told him to get someone to mop up the blood. The guard called the cleaning woman and she got rid of the blood. After she left their room, Aysha broke into tears.

"I don't want to stay here Sams. I wanna leave as soon as possible. I don't want a vacation," she cried.

"Yeah Ash, we are gonna leave this town soon. Maybe tomorrow. Let me go and confirm the tickets. Are you sure you can stay alone while I go and confirm the tickets?" asked Sami.

"To leave this cursed city? Sure," replied Aysha.

But Aysha's stern reply soon started to fade away as soon as Sami left the hotel. She was hearing strange noises the moment Sami left the room. She felt that someone was spying on her. She pulled the curtains and locked the door. Still she felt that she was being spied on. She turned on the radio to distract her mind and turned back towards the closet to pack her bags. As soon as she turned her back someone turned the radio off. She turned back but saw no one there. Then a strange voice began calling her from the bathroom. She searched for a weapon but found none. After searching for a while, maybe for ten seconds when each and every second seemed like ages, she found a paperweight. She picked it up and approached the bathroom. As she entered the bathroom, the voice stopped calling her. But the feeling that a pair of sinister eyes was watching her still haunted her. Suddenly she felt that the pair of eyes was just behind her. She quickly turned and threw the paperweight shouting, "Leave me alone!" All she heard was the cracking of the mirror and all she saw was her distorted face on the broken glass. She broke down into tears.

Soon Sami returned and searched for Aysha. Failing to find her in the room he knocked on the door of the bathroom. But when he heard no answer from Aysha, he opened the door and found her crying softly on the floor.

"Pack your bags Ash. We are leaving tomorrow morning," he ordered.

For the whole afternoon, the two friends hardly exchanged a word between them. At last Sami broke the silence.

"I am going out to buy a pack of Bensons. Would you like to join me?"

"Yeah sure! I need a walk," Aysha replied.

When they two crossed the street in front of the hotel they found two very familiar figures coming towards them. Aysha and Sami saw that the figures were theirs. It seemed that the two persons in front of them were their identical twins. Suddenly the girl from the bar appeared behind their look-alikes. She smiled at Aysha and Sami and took out a sword. She looked at the sword, smiled at them again and with one slash chopped the heads off their look-alikes. They were so close that blood gushed out of the two decapitated beings and covered their faces. Both of them closed their eyes, shocked. When they opened their eyes, they saw that it was not blood but water that had pooled on the pavement from the rain the previous night and a speeding car had splashed them. And most importantly there were no twins, no girl from the bar, and certainly no sword.

"That was a weird hallucination!" said Sami to himself in an extremely soft voice.

Aysha nodded.

Sami looked at her, surprised, and asked "You also saw that?"

Aysha nodded again, wordlessly.

When they went back to the hotel room Aysha got back to packing her bags. She looked at all the clothes she had brought with her and thought of all the many plans she had made for this trip. She felt sad and also relieved at leaving London so early. She opened the closet to get her clothes; she noticed an old wooden box. She hadn't seen it before. She knelt down and took the lid off.

"Hey, Sams, look!" she called.

Sami quickly ran to her and looked into the box. An old revolver was inside. It was old, metallic black, and it was loaded.

"Where did this come from?" asked Sami startled and amazed.

"Maybe the person who stayed here before us left it here," said Sami giving the answer to his question himself.

Aysha pulled the revolver from the box and stared at it for some time. The revolver seemed to attract her a great deal.

"Ash, leave the gun where it was and get back to packing." The gun seemed to have left no impression on Sami. But Aysha, no matter how much she tried, couldn't keep her eyes off the gun. Sami was packing his bags and paid no attention to what Aysha was doing. After packing up, he looked at Aysha and saw the gun pointed at him.

BOOM!!

The revolver was loaded. The gunshot split Sami's head into two parts. The right part was fully smashed. One of his eyes popped out and hit the wall behind him. Some parts of his skull and the brain also covered the wall.

Knock! Knock!

"Who is it?" asked Aysha taking her eyes off the dead bloody Sami.

"It's Officer Roland. You left your purse at the station, Ma'am."

"Okay! I'm coming," said Aysha very slowly.

But Aysha didn't move to open the door. Instead she stared towards the window. There she could see that the girl from the bar was standing outside. She sported an evil smile of satisfaction on her face. A smile also spread on Aysha's face. Aysha slowly pointed the revolver at her ear and held the trigger.

BANG!

"Your drinks," said the bartender.

Aysha gave a stir and saw a glass of orange juice mixed with brandy in front of her. She exhaled a sigh of relief. "But why did such a wild dream strike me?" she thought. Was it a prophecy of some kind? Was it a vision of things to come? When the world is inching each day towards World War III, bloodshed and death are becoming a common phenomenon. She thought over the matter again and wondered what a dreadful and hopeless world it was becoming.

Sami finished his vodka and ordered another shot. Aysha held her drink and got submersed in her thoughts without taking a single sip.

Whispered Recall
Hildibrand Sarker

"Man is Born Free, but Chained Everywhere"

This vicious realization confronts someone in a question of liberty and soul. It involves a right that we, as human beings, have come to expect since the day that mankind was born.

***

The collective writings in this script, that I am afraid to identify as what others would call a *piece of literature*, are simply reflections of an individual who demanded too little from life. All he sought was a small breathing space around him, a view of the autumn sky through his tiny window, the devotion of an uninterrupted personal hour to listen in to the melodies of nature, and time to walk into the woods in silence. Perhaps these are the most precious elements on today's earth, which was unknown to this deprived man. So he had to pay the price in exchange for his expectations, that's worth his so called feat in life later on.

Betrayed, defeated, a fugitive seeks out a secret place to hide. A place for respite, to retreat perhaps to revive in the spirit of the eminent verse, "You don't live with what happened in your life but with what you do with it."

Dear Audience this is where the story begins. A new journey towards the unknown, following the turns of a river's sandy bank – into memory, or toward the uncertainties of the future. It's just a beginning. It's about a rendezvous, a call for resurrection. Hence, the title, "Whispered Recall."

17th September, 05

A tiny apartment on the third floor of a four storied old-fashioned building facing the east, at the middle of a cosmopolitan city. A combination drawing and dining room at the entrance is just large enough to hold only the most necessary furniture. A passage so narrow that two people could not walk side-by-side runs towards two rooms on the opposite side of the apartment. The one on the right has been arranged to accommodate Partho. The other belongs to the owner of the apartment.

Despite the modest size of the room, it proudly holds a grand window that displays the gorgeous blue sky of autumn. Partho adores the view and sits by the window on a divan facing the east. It's a beautiful evening that approaches in silence, the mystical twilight casts its net over the horizon, and a band of swifts flee hurriedly towards destiny. Eyes fixed on the panorama, Partho holds the same posture without any movement, as if he has been into a state of meditation for a century.

Obsessed within his lost world, Partho fails to notice the presence of someone standing behind him, who has been observing his state with great compassion.

It is Reba, who possesses the apartment and who is a physician by profession, and who has always been more than just an aunt to Partho. A person with an individuality that reflects in her comportment, one who can easily be differentiated from others by her warmth. Unfortunately, Partho's rendezvous with this person, a few times only, always had to be in moments of turmoil in his life. She always played the role of a true shepherd, and Partho despite his adamant attitude obeyed her like a little boy.

He feels that Reba has been quite successful in turning this tiny apartment into a sanctuary for lost souls like him. It is an ideal place to take refuge. To add to its flavor, her motherly affection makes the whole place feel like a true home.

" . . . . And how are you feeling today, Partho," Reba asks. Startled, Partho turns, sees her and sighs in response.

A glimpse of twilight touches her face through the window, she looks amber as if she has just swum off the shore into the sundown horizon. "How long have you been here," Partho asks. "It's a beautiful evening, isn't it" Reba always asks questions in return, Partho sighs again, wordless. "Partho, have you ever seen how the sun goes down, while standing in the middle of a vast field covered with ripened crops, all alone," Reba enquires.

"No," replies Partho in a submissive fashion.

"It's like a colorful painting, no not just an ordinary painting, it's a moment of realizing the truth, where the infinite firmament embraces the terrain," Reba pauses.

"Truth?" Partho asks mysteriously.

"Yes, the answer that you've been in search of all these years. The new dimensions of life that you haven't yet discovered," replies Reba.

On the stereo, Hariprasad Chowrasia has begun playing his flute to a tune. Evening in Raga "*kalyan,*" it plays on to bridge the material world with the virtual one.

Night falls.

The next day.

Partho spends a very busy day. He needs to get a few things straight to safeguard his life. After all, it's the only thing that's left now. By the time he returns to the apartment, the twilight has already disappeared beneath the wings of darkness. Partho sits by his favorite place, looks into the darkness with tired eyes. He thinks about what someone had told him the other day, something about the facets of life. "Is there anything left or that should be, in life?" Partho interrogates himself. The darkness whispers to him, in anticipation, "Loser." "Who says that?" Partho shouts back. "Your tea," Mahin approaches with a mug of tea, deposits it on the table behind the divan where Partho was sitting, pulls out a chair kept aside the table and sits facing Partho.

Dear Audience, allow me to introduce this third character "Mahin." If you can recall, this place is considered a sanctuary of many lost ones, a shelter for the nomad. Mahin, a plain hearted boy from the countryside, is around twenty-three or four years in age. He has been in this house for a few years. He has dreams in his eyes again, dreams that he had once lost. Mahin, and his parents back at the village, had cherished hopes of an accomplished life. But the world had left him, along with rest of the household, to starve. It had played a cruel game of fortune, and exposed him stark naked, throwing off the last piece of rag that covered his humiliating poverty. Reba had picked him up and sheltered him like a goddess of salvation.

Partho, somewhat bashfully, picks up the mug and gulps the steaming tea to the last drop. A few moments later, he notices the silence around him and initiates a chat with his companion.

"Mahin, I've been thinking of traveling to places I haven't been before," Partho proposes. Mahin, knowing the recent state of Partho's life, can't disapprove of the idea and his eyes give a positive response.

A few days later.

A few days passed in between, not much of activities to be involved with. This is not the kind of life Partho is usually used to. He feels the urge for mobility. Besides it's a weekend. He sets off towards nowhere very early in the morning, alone.

He travels for about an hour or two before he realizes that he had come out of his residence absent mindedly, not letting anyone know where he would go. It had almost reached afternoon, the place around him seemed to have an ancient look, streets with fewer crowds and traffic, the shops and houses seeming to be left at the same state since being erected, pretty old fashioned in their architectural design, roads were comparatively narrow to the ones in the city side.

He takes the sidewalk and moves forward at a slow pace. He reaches the end of the city, the southern part that comes up to a river called *Buriganges* that flows for ages as a witness to all time. A signpost struck on a wall displays the name of the place that reads "Narayandia." The name reminds one that once there was an ancient landlord named Narayan. Partho discovers a very old cemetery surrounded with thick high walls. A towering and massive welcoming gateway made of bricks faces the south. "Quite a place for the souls to rest," Partho whispers to himself. The whole place is covered with the graves of people from all walks of life and times, of all castes and classes. Laid in the same earth and dust, equally.

A truth unearthed.

That night Partho cannot sleep well. He seems to be in a state of imprisonment. Held by the distress and concerns that he carries forward from the place he visited during the day. At the dead part of night, while walking by the corridor, with eyes fixed on the floor, he repeatedly utters a part of a verse over and over " . . . and I have miles to go before I sleep."

A few months later.

A month or two later Partho, while checking his e-mails on the Internet, is surprised to received an e-mail from a sender with a mysterious identity. The mail reads "Partho . . . Do I contradict myself. Well, maybe I do. I am multitude. Catch me if you can. See you again." The mail was signed with an illusionary name, "Mayabini."

Partho stares at the mail for sometime, he has no idea what this mysterious e-mail means or who has sent it. But the next moment he is filled with a sudden thrill inside and feels like he has known the sender for ages, perhaps in his previous life. The one he has been in search of – all through his life, the path he had been traveling all by himself with hope. Partho finally replies with one of his favorite quotes, "Standing by the fence, I see you. Your smile your, wondrous smile, I bow deeply . . . . "

And that was the beginning of revival. Partho realizes that this is his call and there is someone out there who can salvage his sinking vessel.

At first he receives the mails once or twice a month. And most of them are verses from Partho's favorite writers. This begins to draw him gradually closer to the mysterious character. The verses are so carefully selected, as if they are only meant for him and have been written only a minute ago.

The edifice built of Partho's belief is so sturdy that on a sweet summer night Partho composes his finest piece of literary work. A poem he dedicates to Maya, a poem that will become one of her fondest possessions. A type of poem -- only one of its kind every written:

Alone like a cloud
Over the relentless misfortunate earth
In the shimmering light of dawn or dusk

I travel above your windowpane, wishing
To see you for the last time
Oh Dear, what a thirst I bore in my heart ever
Which turned me into a love vapor.

Gently flows the river, I beheld in my eyes
Down the valley, once we used to be

Hand in hand, side-by-side, eyes fixed in eyes
Made us walk a thousand miles
Oh Dear what a thirst I had in my eyes ever
Which turned me into a blue river.

Listen to the whistling wind, blowing on a sweet summer night
It's the song my voice once entertained
Those sleepless nights, the romantic silence
That expressed our perseverance
Oh Dear what a thirst I bore in my voice ever
Which turned me into a wind of whimper.

When you see the mountain – and rain behind its brow
Think of me, standing for ages, awaiting
And I am covered with primrose, lily and shy daffodils
Once, you had them all in your garden of paradise
Oh Dear what a thirst I bore in my gesture ever
Which turned me into a mountain tear.

Go to the valley and call out for me
Listen to the rhythm of echo – that is me
Once there, on the widening meadow
We frolicked, we danced and we laughed together as we grew
Now it's lost and can never be found under heaven or sky
Oh Dear, now it's only a memory and my cry

If you ever, anymore, look at the stars when midnight is due
You'll find me as a lonely sparkle gazing at you
There was a time, when we climbed the heights o're the hills
Together we counted all the stars, blew our wishes up to the celestial view
Oh Dear what a thirst I bore in your wishes then
Which turned me into a bohemian

You were the goddess of love to me
Taught me how and what love should be
As you touched, smiled and looked into my eyes
Love bloomed under the rain washed skies

Maya, My dear,
This is my song and my final urge to you
Come by my side, as
A cloud or a river,
A star or mountain
If you ever believed in Re-incarnation.

Partho receives mails more frequently. Now they contain something more than just verses. It is about a new relationship. Everything seems to happen as an upshot of a well-organized plan driving on as smooth as a silk. Soon it was time for the curtain raiser, the end of the masquerade. Partho, to his greatest surprise, learned that the mysterious maiden was someone from his hometown, who now lived on the other side of the world from him.

Partho has found the truth, finally -- an e-mail that has turned his life around, to a new direction. Miracles do occur in every shape and form, and miracles are able to adapt technologically as well, it seems.

Hmm ….. Interesting.

WEEK FOUR:
DRAMA:

A conflict is made up of a series of crises, straining points in the conflict that cause the realignment of forces or some change in the character. The plot is created by the selection and ordering of these crises. In each scene's internal crisis, an action is taken or not taken, or a decision is made or not made knowingly by the character. The plot is created by the selection and ordering of these crises. – Irwin R. Blacker, screenwriter, teacher, novelist, and television documentary writer.

Written in a team:
- ❖ The first scene of a screenplay
- ❖ The first act of a full-length play
- ❖ A short [short] one act play

When creating your dramatic scene remember the advice of author Carol Whitely:
- Move the story forward
- Move the main character closer to or further away from the goal.
- Add to the readers'/viewers' understanding of the character.
- Have a beginning, middle, and an end.
- Show how the characters involved feel.
- Be compelling—contain either conflict or the foreshadowing of it, or show an unexpected alliance between opponents.
- Keep viewers eager to learn what happens next.

To contend for the highest grade your team must -- *complete the Treatment and Outline sheet and write a 4 – 5 minute scene. In addition, if we have time, you should be ready to act out or table-read your script.*

WAR FIELD
Idrak Hossain

<u>Characters</u>:

1. Hauus: Protagonist plus the antagonist. A man of twenty-seven.
2. James: A friend of Hauus. A man who likes to live on the edge. A personality of Hauus.
3. Twain: Another friend of Hauus . A very introverted person. A personality and also the reality of Hauus.
4. Heathfield: Army commander
5. Carie: Hauus' girlfriend
6. Jovan: The president
7. Some other minor characters

<u>Stage</u>:

The stage is divided into two parts. One half is used mainly for the real action and the other half is used for the actions that are occurring in the characters' minds. Throughout the play the spotlight plays a vital role by moving to and fro between the two sections. The stage either becomes completely dark at times or almost dark where the dim light shows the physical outline of a character on one side of the state while there is action taking place on the other segment of the stage.

Scene: 1

(Someone is lying on a bed. The whole room is dark save the fact that a spotlight is on Hauus who is standing. He is clad in an army uniform. Suddenly he puts his hand on his waist and falls down. As soon as he falls down, the person on the bed gives a shrill cry and jumps up. We see that the figure on the bed is also Hauus. The whole room is lit up and we see that it is a hospital room. A light from the window shows that it is now morning.)

Hauus: *(Sighs)* The same old dream. I don't know why it comes flashing back all the time! *(He lays down again, closes his eyes and tries to sleep.)*

James: Morning Hausi! Wake up! (Hands him a cigarette) Here, suck on this. *(He lights the cigarette for Hauus.)*

Hauus: *(Blowing out a few rings of smoke)* Man, how long do I have to stay here!

James: As long as you need. The doctors have to release you with a certificate, right? As long as you stay here, your chances of surviving increase. So, the choice is yours.

Twain: C 'mon Hausi, you want to live now, right. You are blessed with a life. You have fought it out. So live on!

Hauus: Yes buddy. Thanks for being with me! Now I have got the inspiration to live on. And I will. *(He takes another drag of the cigarette and seems to get lost in his thoughts.)*

[Scene 1 ends]

Scene: 2
(The spotlight points at a door in a pitch-dark room. Some men are knocking at the door. The door opens and they enter the room. Some police officers are also there with them.)

Voice 1:   Call the Doc at once!

Voice 2:   I think we can still save Hauus.

Twain: Call the Doc! The President is in critical condition.

(Hauus moans as everyone is attending the President. A lady doctor comes, checks the president's wrist, declares him dead and attends Hauus.)

Doc: He is bleeding profusely. Get him to the OT at once otherwise we will lose him also.

(Hauus is taken to the OT. The doctor comes out after 30 minutes.)

Doc: He is out of danger now but he might need blood. Do you know his family members?

Voice 3:   Nope, Doc.

Doc: But we need to admit him.

Voice 3:   He's the president's bodyguard. I can sign for him.

(Hauus is taken out of the OT and placed in his room. At the break of day he wakes up with a cry.)

Hauus: *(Sighs)* The same old dream. I don't know why it comes flashing back all the time!

[Scene 2 ends]

Scene 3

(The president is coming out of the conference. He is about to enter his limo. A gunshot is heard and the president falls down. Many people gather around him. Another gunshot is heard and Hauus falls down. The crowd speaks as one, and then there are single, anonymous, voices.)

Crowd: The president is shot! The president is shot!

Anony. 1:   Let's pick him up and take him to the hospital. We can still save him.

Anony. 2:   Hold the car.

(They call the car and carry the president inside the car.)

Anony. 3:   His guard has also been shot.

Hauus: Don't worry about me! Save the president! Save the nation.

Anony. 4:   Carry him off, too!

(Hauus is pulled inside the car. The room darkens. The spotlight points at a door in a pitch-dark room. Some men are banging at the door. The door opens and they enter the room. Some police officers are also there with them.)

[Scene 3 ends]

Scene 4

(The president is in a conference room. Hauus is talking over the earphone.)

Hauus: It's almost over

James: How long will it take?

President: We have to increase taxes. The people don't have the slimmest idea that only 20 percent of the money is going to be used for the war.

Senator 1:   But Mr. President the people will oppose it for sure. Don't you think it will lead to a revolution?

President: No because we'll be imposing indirect taxes.

Senator 2:   Well if you say so then it's done.

James: Is he coming out?

Hauus: Yes

(The president is coming out of the conference building. He is about to enter his limo. A gunshot is heard and the president falls down. Many people gather round him. Another gunshot is heard and Hauus falls down.)

Hauus: Don't worry about me! Save the president! Save the nation.

[Scene 4 ends]

Scene 5

(A dark room. The spotlight falls on one corner of the room where we can see Carrie clearly but only a part of Hauus.)

Carrie: I am extremely sorry Hauus but this thing cannot go on any longer.

Hauus: *(Sobbing)* But Carrie…5 years, can nothing be done?

Carrie: No, Hauus. I think it's all over…I am extremely sorry Hauus but it's all over.

(Carrie walks off the stage. The whole room is lit up again. We see Twain, James and Hauus addressing a crowd. Hauus is staring up and wondering.)

James: *(Softy)* Get back to the scenario Hausi.

(Hauus stirs and addresses the crowd.)

James: This is not us against him. It's the nation against him.

Hauus: We are going to start it comrades but I can guarantee you that soon the whole nation will join hands with us.

(The crowd cheers and everyone holds his fists up.)

James: After we pull down the top ranked official then we are going to get them each -- man after man. Pig after pig, and slaughter them. We are paying the money and he is taking it all. They are making themselves rich. Comrades the time has come to unite and become WE. WE don't need any hierarchy. We need a leader. And soon we will make sure that the nation will become WE. Today is the big day!

Twain: *(Softly)* I think it's your time to leave Hausi.

Hauus: Right you are.

James: Now, Tom, you will bring down the president. What ever you do just make sure that the bullet does not miss his brain. And Mark your job is to shoot Hauus, not kill him. No matter what, Hauus needs to survive. *(Turning to Hauus)* I am sorry Hausi but you need to take a bullet. You are the president's bodyguard. If you don't take any bullet then the police will question you.

Hauus: *(To the crowd)* Don't worry about me Comrades. If I pass away tonight, then I'll be a martyr AND I WILL BE PROUD TO BE ONE.

(The crowd cheers. The spotlight falls on one side of the stage. Hauus is talking over his earphone.)

Hauus: It's almost over

[Scene 5 ends]

Scene 6

(Heathfield is lying in a pool of blood. Hauus is trembling a bit. Twain is also a bit shaky. James is holding a dagger in his hand.)

James: Aaaaaaaaaaah! One bloody hierarchy obsessed S.O. B. is dead. That's a good way to start a big mission.

Twain: *(Shaky)* James, what will happen if we get caught?

James: Listen, boy, what do you want? You want a revolution or you want these white-collar servants of ours to rule over us? If we get caught, then more Twains, Hauuses, and Jameses, will pop up. The servants of our servants can only imprison or hang us. But they cannot stop the revolution. It is running down the blood of a few thousands now. Soon it will infect millions.

(Hauus was looking at the dead Heathfield.)

Hauus: *(Shaky)* You remember how we felt when he tried to kill us in Vietnam?

James: Yes, Hausi, and that is why this bloody bastard has to pay us with his blood and the blood of his family members.

[Scene 6 ends]

Scene 7

(Hauus is sleeping. Carrie appears in his dreams)

Hauus: Carrie have you ever wondered what the world means to me without you?

(Carrie turns around, maybe in fright, to face Hauus and utter these words:)

Carrie: Hauus, I have to tell you something very important.

Hauus: Me too!! *(Saying this he brings out the ring from his pocket.)*

Carrie: I think we have to pull down the curtains, Hauus. I am going to marry Nick next week!

Hauus: WHAT?

(Hauus puts the ring back into his pocket. Carrie turns around the very next moment.)

Carrie: Yes!!!!

(Hauus wakes up, pants, stirs a little and goes back to sleep again.)

Heathfield: So you are still not weaned yet! Listen bloody bastard, I am here to command and you to follow. Let's draw the communication line, ME- order, YOU- follow. Any questions in between and your balls will be juggling in my hand. Lead your men to the 11th regiment. I'll send my back up within 2 hours. Any questions?

Hauus   *(Softly)* No sir.

Heathfield: W-H-A-T?

Hauus: NOTHING SIR. NO QUESTIONS!

Heathfield: Good. Otherwise your balls would be bouncing on the ping-pong table!

(Hauus, Twain and James crawl on the ground with guns.)

James: Listen to me Hauus. This is the biggest bluff of the millennium. That bloody bastard has screwed us. It's been three whole freaking hours. Where is that bastard's back up?

(They get up. Hauus gets shot in the chest and hits the ground. The sleeping Hauus wakes up.)

Hauus: (Sighing) Bloody hierarchy obsessed fool. Count your minutes!

(The bell rings. Hauus opens the door. James and Twain are at the door.)

James: Ready Hausi?

Hauus: You bet!

Twain: So let's get going. Today is the day!!

Hauus: Yes.

(The light dims. They go to Heathfield's apartment and ring the bell. Heathfield opens the door and is surprised to see them. They rush in and James stabs Heathfield.)

James: Aaaaaaaaaaah! One bloody mother of a hierarchy-obsessed son on a bitch is dead. A good way to start a big mission!

[Scene 7 ends]

(Scene 8)

(Hauus walks into a bar. He sits at a table where James and Twain are already sitting. He orders a mug of beer.)

Hauus: Hey waiter a mug of beer here!

James: Won't you treat us Hausi?

Hauus: Who are you? Do I know you people?

(James and Twain look at each other and laugh.)

Twain: C'mon Hausi, treat us.

Hauus: Hey waiter two more mugs of beer here.

(The waiter puts both mugs of beer in front of Hauus.)

Hauus: Why the hell are you putting both beers in front of me? Have you gone blind?

Waiter: But, Sir, you are the only person here! And you have ordered them.

Hauus: *(In amazement to James and Twain both)* Who are you people?

James and Twain: WE ARE YOU!

(The light is dimmed to almost dark. When the light returns we see Hauus sitting alone and hear the words "We are you" echoing. The light is again dimmed to almost complete darkness and in the dark the audience still hears the words "We are you." The light is turned on again and we see Hauus in the hospital room, still smoking the same cigarette. He is almost finished. Then the room turns completely dark and we see Hauus addressing the crowd and saying James's words. We cannot see Hauus but we hear Hauus' voice. We only see the back of the character. We don't see Hauus because on stage it is not possible to show Hauus on bed and also addressing the crowd both at the same time. The characters are shown with spotlights. Then the spotlight moves a little and we see a man, clad in Hauus' clothes shooting him when everyone is attending the president. Then the spotlight moves a little and we again see Hauus pulling the dagger out of Heathfield. Then the spotlight shifts once again and we see Hauus talking to himself in the war field. We can only see the back of the characters. The light is dimmed and on the other side of the room, we see the outline of Hauus sitting on his bed. The light gets turned on again).

Hauus: It's a wonder what we humans are capable of doing and what restricts us from what we are. We can hold the whole world in our hand and again we let it drift through our fingers like sand. The irony is we can dictate the world and another's life, but we do not know what life really is. Life is like a war field where we fight for our survival by killing others for other's interest without knowing what our destination is.

MEET THE WRITERS

It is [the writer's] privilege to help man endure by lifting his heart, by reminding him of the courage and honor and hope and pride and compassion and pity and sacrifice, which have been the glory of his past.

--

William Faulkner

Creative Writing in English
A special course for Bangladesh

Instructor: Dr. Patrick T. Dougherty
Department of Global Communication
University of Hyogo
1-1-53#10 Shinzaike Honmachi, Himeji, Hyogo 670-0092, Japan
Phone and Fax: 0792-92- 8808
E-mail: pdougherty@shse.u-hyogo.ac.jp
ct180@hotmail.com

The desire to write grows with writing.
–Erasmus

COURSE DESCRIPTION

Creative Writing in English will provide an opportunity for students to hone their creative writing skills as well as provide a student-centered environment for English language immersion. Students will explore and develop their own ideas through the medium of creative writing. Students will read, write, and share their creative endeavors and providing constructive advice to their peers. The participants in the course will become a small community of writers, eager to compose, share, read, hear, and support.

COURSE GOALS

Students will learn and practice skills that help them craft unique and thoughtful work in English. They will sharpen their critical reading skills through reading, discussion, and writing assignments and will learn the conventions of critique and collaboration. They will maintain a portfolio of revised work and they will submit selected pieces of their creative work to a course literary book.

SPECIFIC COURSE OBJECTIVES FOR THE STUDENTS

Students will:
1. Write creatively and expressively in English
2. Use the appropriate vocabulary for critique
3. Use appropriate literary devices
4. Define the unique characteristics of poetry, fiction, plays, and nonfiction
5. Experiment with a variety of genres
6. Use appropriate pre-writing strategies
7. Develop ideas into draft form
8. Proofread, edit, and revise
9. Present as individuals, in pairs, and small groups
10. Give critiques in a constructive and respectful manner

SPECIFIC COURSE OBJECTIVES FOR THE INSTRUCTOR

To have students grow in confidence in their own ability to be creative, insightful, understanding, and helpful in an English language medium.

To collect enough brilliant examples of student creative work to make a course literary booklet to serve as a permanent reminder for the students of the experience of taking the course and to exhibit their talent to the wider community.

COURSE ORGANIZATION

Study and writing will be organized around the following genres:

1. Biographical or autobiographical sketches
2. Poetry
3. Short stories
4. Plays
5. Multimedia productions (if possible)

A range of activities will be included under each of these genres. However, in all settings serious attention will be given to the stages of the writing process: drafting, revising, editing, and presentation. Students will be expected to keep a reading/writing journal.

CONTENT OF THE COURSE

Creative endeavors flow from the student's knowledge and experience; therefore the course will not simply focus on technique, but will include the following two components:

a. Production: exploration, development, and expression of ideas through writing and the importance of reflection in this process.

b. Critique: reflecting on their own writing, responding critically to published writing as well as their peers' writing; participation in the interactive process between writer and audience.

TEXTS

Select examples of genre writings and creations will be provided in Xeroxed format for the students.

EVALUATION

Grades will be determined by a point system. Grades will be given for assignments done either in or outside of class. Aspects of grading will incorporate the mandated systems of the host institution(s). This might include a midterm examination and a final examination. As projected, students should expect to produce and be graded on these creative items (some of which will be completed individually and others as a team):

A biographical sketch
An autobiographical sketch
Two poems
One short story
One single act play or video piece

And also these items:

Journal entries
Literary critiques
Participation in class activities

And possibly:

A midterm examination (based on examples of the genre pieces)
A final examination (also based on examples of the genre pieces)

DAILY AGENDA

A day-to-day agenda of activities will be created for the course after finalization of the time, dates, and students number for the course is made. This will be provided to the participating students on the first day of the course, or very soon thereafter.

Printed in the United States
By Bookmasters